THE SHIPBROKERS' MANUAL
VOLUME 1

THE SHIPBROKERS' MANUAL
VOLUME 1

COMPILED BY THE INSTITUTE OF CHARTERED SHIPBROKERS

LONDON

LLOYD'S OF LONDON PRESS LTD.

Legal Publishing & Conferences Division,
26-30 Artillery Lane, Bishopsgate, London E1 7LX.

1983

©

THE INSTITUTE OF CHARTERED SHIPBROKERS

ISBN 0-907432-59-X

Printed in Great Britain by
Holmes & Sons (Printers) Limited, Andover, Hampshire

FOREWORD

This series of shipping manuals, which I commend to you, is a further endeavour of our Institute to fulfil aims of our Royal Charter "To educate, to devise and improve means for testing the qualification of candidates for admission to the professional membership of the Institute of Chartered Shipbrokers by examination in theory and practice".

The manuals are, therefore, a realization in part of these aims and are the ideal compendium for students and tutors studying for our professional examination as well as being an updating of knowledge to all nationally and internationally who "go down to the sea in ships".

They encompass the great experience of many very eminent men of shipping whose spoken words have long been respected, transformed into the lasting written words for the future benefit of all, they will ever be a basis for development in time to come.

The complete series, which will be four volumes, has been a tremendous task for our Education Committee, who have planned and organized the contributors in all the sections; to all these men the shipping industry owes a debt of gratitude which can only be repaid by all of us striving to improve our knowledge, and our industry; the consolation being that imparted knowledge never diminishes learning's store.

Grateful thanks must also be extended to the Trustees of our Educational Trust who support this major project.

To all who read and digest the words of wisdom contained herein I wish you well, and hope understanding will result in an improved Shipping Fraternity.

NORMAN FORSTER
JULY 1983

CONTENTS

PAGE

TABLE OF STATUTES

TABLE OF CASES

CHAPTER 1

AN EXAMINER'S VIEW OF CANDIDATES

The contents of this book prepare students for the various examinations of the Institute as far as the factual side is concerned but an aspect which is rarely covered is that of answer preparation. No doubt most people have their personal opinion of examiners and the fact that they are human hardly enters into their calculation. Nevertheless, there is an art in presenting an examination paper and the object of this short chapter is to give the students some idea of the examiner's point of view. A paper which is well presented goes a long way to putting the examiner in a good frame of mind and, in case you think that papers should only be marked when "of sound mind", I must point out that in some examinations there are well over 150 papers to be marked. It is obvious that a well laid out paper will stand out and make the task much easier.

The first object must be to write clearly. It is not given to us all to have very legible writing, especially when in a hurry to answer a long paper, but it is utterly pointless to set down facts and opinions, however accurate, if no one can read them! Some papers are virtually unintelligible and, although all examiners make an extra effort in such cases, it is not always possible to decipher the meaning with accuracy. The candidate is therefore in danger of losing marks due to lack of neatness of presentation and for content. There are usually several marks to be gained on every paper for presentation and it is folly to throw such a bonus away when it can mean the difference between pass and failure.

If we assume that the writing is neat and readable, the next requirement is to lay out the answers in some semblance of order so that it is quite clear which questions are being attempted. When there are alternatives, which is the case in all papers, some of the questions are similar in content and failure to state clearly which question is being answered could result in misunderstanding. It is not, however, necessary to repeat the question which only wastes time and gains no extra marks. Merely to use the question number should be sufficient and a space should be left between answers for clarity. Where several parts exist to one question, these will usually be designated by (a) (b) (c) or possibly (i) (ii) (iii) and such divisions should be clearly shown in the answers.

In some papers, short factual replies are called for and where this is so, elaboration is not only unnecessary but unwise. The examiner does not wish to plough through extraneous matter when he has a large number of papers still to mark.

Shipbroking being largely a practical profession necessitates more lengthy replies to some questions, perhaps expressing an opinion rather than a "right" or "wrong" situation. The best marks will be earned by the students who set out their reasoning clearly and without frills and, needless to say, if the opinion stated does not agree with that of the examiner it will not necessarily result in lower marks. If, however, the explanation is so involved and "woolly" the point may be totally lost when the paper is marked, with obvious consequences. Therefore remember to keep answers clear and to the point, eliminating all words that are not required because, provided you pack all the relevant material into your answer in a coherent manner, you will gain the best possible marks.

When the question of calculations arise such as in laytime statements and voyage estimates, it pays to show your method—*provided such figures are clear*. A jumble of sums spread over rough paper in a haphazard manner often cause the examiner more headaches than the actual answer and are therefore best thrown away unless you are specifically asked to submit them. While for laytime calculations absolute accuracy is essential, it is not possible to be totally accurate arithmetically with voyage estimating because of the inability to state distances exactly and to make totally accurate calculations for such as weather delays. Here the examiner is again looking for system and, above all, the ability to be methodical so that no item is left out of the estimate. Here again clarity is of the utmost importance where figures are involved so do not try to hide ignorance by illegibility. Examiners have also been students in the past and are well aware of such methods!

Probably the biggest single "crime" committed by students is failure to read and/or comprehend the question. You may find this difficult to believe but it is a truism and one questions whether a student who cannot read and understand such problems should be let loose on freight contracts worth millions of pounds. The papers now allow 10 minutes reading time in addition to that allowed for the examination and good use should be made of this time to read the entire paper, choose which of the alternative questions you intend to take and then re-read each question as you attempt it. If you do not fully understand what the examiner is driving at, DO NOT answer the question however easy you think it is.

Most papers also carry compulsory questions and these mean exactly what they say. Failure to attempt them will result in failure and therefore they should be answered first if possible. If you feel nervous (and believe me everybody does, however cool they may appear) it may be a good idea to attempt one of the choice questions about which you are confident just to help you into the mood but do not delay tackling the compulsory, and therefore probably more difficult, questions early in the paper because your time may run out earlier than you think and valuable marks thus be thrown away. In this connection, it is totally useless to answer more than the required number of questions because, unlike backing a horse both ways, you do not improve your chances of success. In fact, the examiner will probably mark you down for not being able to count!

It is perhaps slightly unorthodox to suggest that students make guesses at answers they do not know but, particularly where a factual reply is called for, it is better to put an answer rather than to leave a blank. In the latter case, you will definitely receive no marks while an "inspired" guess could be very valuable in the final total.

CHAPTER 2

SALE OF GOODS

The law relating to contracts for the sale of goods has been codified in the Sale of Goods Act 1979, which consolidates the amendments to the Sale of Goods Act 1893. The 1979 Act came into force on Jan. 1, 1980. The 1893 Act is repealed with the exception of section 26 which deals with the effect on goods of writs of execution. The contract of sale is one of the oldest and most necessary of mercantile transactions.

The Act defines a Contract of Sale of Goods as:—

> "A contract where the seller transfers or agrees to transfer the property in goods to the buyer for a money consideration, 'the price' ".

There are two kinds of contract dealt with in this definition:

1. A sale and transfer of property, i.e. an Executed Contract.

2. An agreement to sell and transfer in the future, i.e. an Executory Contract.

A contract of sale may be either an agreement to sell or it can be an actual sale.

The contract of sale provides for the property in the goods to be transferred from the seller to the buyer and this contract is known as a sale. But when the transfer of property in the goods is to take place at a future time, or is to be subject to some condition which will be fulfilled at an agreed future time, then this contract is called an "Agreement to Sell".

The law as applied to the sale of goods is governed by the Sale of Goods Act 1979, section 4 of which provides, with certain exceptions, that the contract of sale may be in any form.

The contract may be oral or in writing or partly oral and partly in writing. The law would appear to be that evidence, oral or written, will be the guiding factor as to whether a contract exists between the two parties. The law on this subject was summarised in the case *Dawson Line* v. *Adler* (1931) Greer, L.J., as follows:—

> "One of the most important rules of law that can be regarded by everybody as a certainty is this—that if people adopt a written form of words to represent their contractual obligations, their contractual obligations will be found in that document, and the Court will not lightly weaken the effect of what they have undertaken by their written words by implying from the document itself any qualification or any implied undertaking that is inconsistent with those written words".

The following are the principal features of the Sale of Goods Act 1979.

Conditions

A condition is a stipulation in a contract which goes to the root of the contract. It is, therefore, an essential part of the contract. Breach of a condition gives rise to a right to treat the contract as repudiated, although the wronged party has an option to treat the breach as a breach of warranty.

The following conditions are *implied* in every contract of sale, subject to any provision to the contrary.

(1) That the seller has a right to sell the goods, commercially and legally.

(2) Where there is a sale by description, that the goods shall correspond with the description.

(3) Where there is a sale by sample as well as by description, that the whole of the goods shall correspond both with the sample and with the description.

(4) Where the purchase is made by description from a seller who deals in goods of that description, that the goods are of a merchantable quality.

(5) Where goods are sold for a particular purpose, either by expression or implication, the goods are reasonably fit for that purpose.

(6) Where the sale is by sample, that:
   (a) the bulk shall correspond with the sample as to quality;
   (b) the buyer shall have a reasonable opportunity to compare the bulk with the sample;
   (c) the goods shall be free from any defect, rendering them unmerchantable, which would not be apparent by a reasonable examination of the sample.

Warranties

A warranty is also a stipulation, but it is not of such importance as to go to the root of the contract, and is collateral to the main purpose of the contract. Unlike a breach of condition, breach of warranty does not give a right of repudiation, but merely a right to damages.

In the absence of agreement to the contrary, the following warranties are implied in every contract of sale:—

(1) That the buyer shall have and enjoy quiet possession of the goods, and

(2) that the goods are free from any charge or encumbrance in favour of any third party, which has not been declared, or made known to the buyer before, or at the time when the contract was made.

The doctrine of "Caveat emptor"

Apart from the implied conditions and warranties previously mentioned, specifically agreed conditions and warranties may be expressed in the contract itself. It is the responsibility of the parties clearly to express their intentions at the inception of the contract, otherwise the Common Law rule of *caveat emptor* applies, which means "let the buyer beware". This doctrine is in contrast to that applicable to insurance contracts which are contracts of the utmost good faith (*uberrimae fidei*).

Terms of a contract

In a contract there are two types of terms, i.e. Express and Implied terms.

Express terms

This term speaks for itself. It is a simple statement that the terms in the contract will be specified in writing. The parties may expressly state every term of their contract with varying degrees of precision or they may simply agree the basic purpose of the contract (express terms) or leave the detailed terms to be deduced from the surrounding circumstances (implied terms).

Implied terms

The general rule is that the parties are presumed to have expressed their intentions fully in the contract. The Courts will only imply additional terms where it is strictly necessary to give effect to the clear intentions of the parties, or where custom or statute requires the implication.

The Court may sometimes import into a contract a term not expressed in it, but necessarily implied. These terms which may be by custom or usage, commercial or otherwise, may be implied.

Again it may be emphasised that it is up to the parties to the contract to specify the nature of their obligations, but if they omit a term which it was their presumed intention to make the basis of their contract, then the Court will imply that term, so as to give "business efficiency" to their contract, where by so doing no inconsistency will arise between the implied term and the terms actually expressed.

By example

The following useful test was laid down by Scrutton in *Reigate* v. *Union Manufacturing Co.* (1918).

> "The first thing is to see what the parties have expressed in the contract; and then an implied term is not to be added because the Court thinks it would have been reasonable to have inserted it in the contract; that is, if it is such a term that it can confidently be said that if at the time the contract was being negotiated someone had said to the parties, 'What will happen in such a case' they would both have replied, 'Of course, so and so will happen; we did not trouble to say that; it is too clear'. Unless the Court comes to some such conclusion as that, it ought not to imply a term which the parties themselves have not expressed".

Contracts for the sale of goods

They are contracts whereby the seller transfers, or agrees to transfer, the "property" in "goods" to the buyer for a consideration called the price.

Property

Property means the complete ownership and should not be confused with custody (when goods are held by a person on behalf of a third party), or "possession" (when goods are merely held with possibly no rights as to custody or property).

Goods

Goods include all chattels personal and include the following types of goods:—

(a) *Existing goods*, which are owned or possessed at the time of the contract of sale; or,

(b) *future goods*, which are to be manufactured or acquired by the seller at some future time after the date of the contract.

The goods may be either:—

(a) *Specific or ascertained goods*, which can be identified and agreed upon at the commencement of the contract; or,

(b) *general or unascertained goods*, which cannot in fact be identified, but are described or referred to by the parties in general terms.

Price

The price may be fixed by the terms of the contract or may be determined by the course of the dealings between the parties. In the absence of either of these provisions the buyer is required to pay a reasonable price, which is determined by the facts.

Performance of the contract

The seller has a duty to deliver the goods to the buyer and likewise the buyer has a duty to accept the goods and to pay the price in accordance with the terms of the contract of sale. The best example of a modification on this rule would be in respect of the giving of credit to the buyer.

It is of course subject to contractual agreement as to whether the buyer has to collect the goods or whether it is for the seller to send them. However, unless it is otherwise agreed it is the responsibility of the seller to pay the costs of putting the goods in a deliverable state. In general, therefore, the basic rules for delivery are:—

1. Whether it is for the buyer to take possession of the goods, or for the seller to send them to the buyer is dependent upon the terms of the contract. Unless agreed otherwise the place for delivery is the seller's place of business, but if the contract is for the sale of specific goods which are known by the parties when the contract is concluded to be in some other place, then that place is the place of delivery.

2. Where under the terms of the contract the seller is bound to send the goods to the buyer, but no time limit is fixed, the seller must send them within a reasonable time.

3. Where the goods, at the time of sale are in the possession of a third person, there is no effective delivery by the seller to the buyer, unless such third person acknowledges to the buyer that he holds the goods on the latter's behalf.

4. Demand or tender of delivery may be treated as ineffectual, unless made at a reasonable hour. What is a reasonable hour is, of course, dependent on fact.

5. Unless otherwise agreed, the expenses of putting the goods into a deliverable state must be borne by the seller.

6. Unless otherwise agreed, where the goods are sent by the seller to the buyer by a route involving sea transit, in circumstances where it is usual to insure, the seller must give such notice to the buyer to enable him to insure the goods during sea transit. If he fails to do so the goods are deemed to be at the seller's risk during such transit.

7. Where the seller of goods agrees to deliver them at a place other than the place of sale, the buyer must, unless agreed to the contrary, assume any risk of deterioration of the goods incidental to such goods during the ordinary course of transit.

Acceptance by the buyer

Acceptance takes place when the buyer:—

    (a) Intimates to the seller that he has accepted the goods; or,

    (b) does any act to the goods which is consistent with the ownership of the seller; or,

    (c) retains the goods, after the lapse of a reasonable time, without intimating to the seller that he has rejected them.

    (d) The buyer is entitled to examine the goods not previously seen, before accepting them. Generally the place of delivery is the place of examination, unless otherwise agreed.

    (e) If the buyer rejects the goods, when entitled to do so, he is not bound to return them to the seller, but only to notify the seller of rejection so as to enable the seller to collect them.

    (f) If the buyer's rejection amounts to a repudiation of the contract the seller has an immediate right of action. The same applies when the buyer keeps the goods for an unreasonable length of time without making his mind up whether to accept or reject the goods.

    In such circumstances the seller's damages will be measured as the amount of loss caused by the wrongful retention.

Rights of the buyer

The buyer has the right, after payment or agreement to pay, whichever the contract allows, to expect delivery of the goods, in accordance with the contract terms. If he does not so secure delivery, he has the right to claim:—

In the event of non-delivery

    (a) To recover the price, if paid; or,

    (b) damages, in accordance with the provisions laid down by the Act; or,

    (c) specific performance of the contract by order of the Court. However, this right will only be granted if damages would not be an adequate remedy.

For breach of condition

He is entitled to reject the goods, but this right of rejection does not apply when:

1. The buyer waives the breach of condition and elects to treat it as a breach of warranty; or,

2. the contract is not severable, and he has accepted the goods, or part of them; or,

3. the contract is for specific goods, and the property has passed to him.

In all three cases mentioned above the breach can only be treated as a breach of warranty.

For breach of warranty

On breach of warranty the buyer can either:

    (a) Set up against the seller the breach of warranty in diminution, or extinction of the price; or,

    (b) maintain an action against the seller for a breach of warranty.

Delivery to a carrier

Where the seller is to send the goods, delivery to a carrier (as agent for the buyer) whether named by the buyer or not, is *prima facie* proper delivery to the buyer. In such cases the seller must make a reasonable contract with the carrier, otherwise the buyer is entitled to refuse to be bound.

Delivery of wrong quantities

General Rules

1. If less than ordered is delivered the buyer may reject the lot; if he does accept the lesser quantity he must pay a proportionately reduced price.

2. If more than ordered is delivered the buyer may reject the lot or may accept the agreed quantity (if this is possible). If he accepts the lot he must pay a proportionately increased price.

3. If goods ordered are mixed with goods not ordered, the buyer may accept those goods ordered and reject the others (if it is at all possible to separate them, if not he must accept or reject the lot).

Rights of seller

The seller has two primary rights against the buyer:—

1. He can require the buyer to accept the goods; and

2. he can require the buyer to pay the price of the goods.

These rights are subject to any conditions expressed in the contract of sale itself.

Except when otherwise agreed, where goods are delivered to the buyer and he refuses to accept them, and he has the right to take this action, he is not bound to return them to the seller. It is sufficient if he intimates to the seller that he refuses to accept them. When the seller is willing and ready to deliver the goods and requests the buyer to take delivery, but the buyer does not within a reasonable time after such request take delivery, the latter is liable to the seller:—

1. For any loss occasioned by his neglect or refusal to take delivery.

2. For a reasonable charge for the care and custody of the goods.

In all cases, subject to agreement otherwise, delivery of the goods and payment of the price are concurrent conditions.

Rights of an unpaid seller against the goods

Unpaid seller

The term includes any person who is in the position of seller, he may not be the owner, e.g., a factor.

The seller remains unpaid so long as any part of the purchase price is outstanding.

Payment by a negotiable instrument is conditional only, i.e. is not effective until the negotiable instrument has been honoured.

The seller may have to contend with two different legal situations.

(a) Where the property has not passed to the buyer.

(b) Where the property has passed to the buyer.

The seller's rights differ in these two cases.

Property which has not passed to buyer

Here the seller may:

(a) Withhold delivery if the price is unpaid or not tendered or if the buyer is insolvent.

(b) If part of the goods have been delivered he may withhold the remainder of the goods.

Property which has passed to buyer

Here the seller has the following rights.

(a) Lien.

(b) Stoppage in transit.

(c) Re-Sale.

Lien

The seller's lien is a right to retain possession of the goods until payment or tender of payment.

A lien arises when:

(a) Goods have been sold on credit and the buyer has become insolvent (whether the period of credit has expired or not).

A lien is lost when

(a) Goods have been delivered to a carrier for transmission to the buyer, without the seller reserving a right of disposal.

(b) The buyer or his agent lawfully obtains possession of the goods.

(c) The seller waives his lien.

The seller may exercise a lien

(a) When in possession merely as agent for the buyer.

(b) Where part delivery has taken place. (The lien extends over the remainder of the goods.)

(c) If the seller breaks his contract while the buyer is solvent he will still be entitled to claim a lien if the buyer subsequently becomes insolvent.

Stoppage in transit

This means a right to stop the goods when they are on their way to the buyer (and after they have left the possession of the seller).

The right arises when;

(a) The goods are in transit, and

(b) the buyer becomes insolvent. (The buyer is insolvent if he has ceased to pay his debts as they fall due or in the ordinary course of business.)

The right of stoppage *in transitu* can only be exercised as long as the goods are in course of transit, and rules for determining the duration of transit are:

(a) Goods are deemed to be in course of transit from the moment they are delivered to a carrier for the purpose of transmission to the buyer, and until the buyer takes delivery from the carrier.

(b) If the buyer obtains delivery of the goods before actual arrival at the appointed destination, the transit is at an end.

Transit ceases when the goods reach their ultimate destination, but not some intermediate destination (unless further instructions are conveyed to the carrier to send them on, in which case transit has ceased).

How stoppage in transit is effected

This is done by the seller:

    (a) Taking possession of the goods or documents of title thereto; or

    (b) giving notice to the carrier of his exercise of the right of stoppage.

If the seller wrongfully stops the goods, e.g., where the buyer is solvent, he is liable for damages for the tort of conversion if the property has passed to the buyer, or for damages for breach of contract if the property has not yet passed to the buyer.

If a carrier wrongfully delivers stopped goods to the buyer he is liable for damages to the seller. If he wrongfully obeys the seller's instructions to stop transit, he is liable for damages to the buyer.

Transit ceases when:

    (a) Goods reach their destination and possession is delivered to the buyer or his agent.

    (b) The buyer or his agent obtains delivery before they reach their destination.

    (c) A carrier wrongfully refuses to deliver the goods to the buyer or his agent.

    (d) The goods have reached their destination and the carrier has notified the buyer that he holds them as his agent.

    (e) Goods are delivered to the master of the buyer's ship, or of a ship which the buyer has chartered.

The seller's right of stoppage in transit is not affected by any sale or other disposition of the goods which the buyer may have made, unless the seller has assented thereto, but where the documents of title have been lawfully transferred to a second buyer, and that buyer in turn transfers all the documents to another person in good faith, and for a valuable consideration by way of a sale, the unpaid seller's right of stoppage in transit is defeated.

If an unpaid seller has exercised his right of lien, or right of stoppage in transit, and resells the goods, the new buyer acquires a good title thereto as against the original buyer who is in default.

The unpaid seller may resell:

   (a) Where the goods are of a perishable nature.

   (b) Where he gives notice to the buyer of his intention to resell, and the buyer does not, within a reasonable time, pay or tender the price.

   (c) Where he expressly reserves a right of resale if the buyer should default.

When does the "property" pass?

It is of extreme importance to determine when the property in the goods, being the subject of a sale contract, actually passes from the seller to the buyer. The reason is that should the goods become lost or damaged before the transaction has been completed then, subject to any other agreement between the parties, the loss will have to be borne by the party in whom the property is vested at the time of the loss or damage. However, this principle will not apply where the actual loss or damage was caused by the fault of the other party.

In a situation where the loss or damage was due to delay in delivery caused by the fault of either party the goods themselves will be at the risk of the party at fault as regards any loss which might not have occurred but for such fault, even though the property has not yet passed.

The rules, however, do not affect the duties or liabilities of either party if he is in the position of bailee of the goods for such other party.

Where the contract does not state when the property or ownership is to pass, the Courts will apply the following rules for ascertaining the intention of the parties.

   (1) When the goods are in a deliverable state, property passes when the contract is made. For example:

      A enters a shop and orders certain goods which are in existence in the shop, ready for delivery and duly priced, to be sent to his house and the price of the goods to be debited to his account. The property passes immediately, although the goods are not delivered until the following day and the account is not settled for three months. This transaction is known as a sale of goods, as opposed to an agreement to sell. For example, there can only be an "agreement to sell" goods which are yet to be manufactured or otherwise acquired by the seller after making the contract. These are known as future goods in the Act.

   (2) When goods need some operation to render them deliverable, property does not pass until this action has been completed and the buyer notified.

(3) When some further operation has to be carried out, such as weighing, measuring or testing, property cannot pass until this process has been completed and the buyer notified.

(4) When goods are actually delivered to the buyer "on approval", or on "sale or return" the property passes to the buyer.

(5) When he signifies his approval or acceptance to the seller or does any other act adopting the transaction.

(6) If he retains the goods without giving notice of rejection beyond the time fixed for the return of the goods, or if no time is fixed, beyond a reasonable time.

Terms of sale

In the shipping business certain terms for the sale of goods have become recognised and when a contract is negotiated on one of these terms, the parties are well aware of the basis of the contract and their responsibilities thereunder.

An international set of rules was introduced in 1953 by the International Chamber of Commerce known as "Incoterms". There are some 1980 amendments.

INCOTERMS

The general purpose of "Incoterms" as introduced was to provide a set of international rules for the interpretation of the major terms used in foreign trade contracts. They were designed for the optional use in business for those who prefer to have certainty of uniform international rules where varied interpretations may be placed on contractual terms in different countries.

It frequently happens that parties to a contract in different countries are not aware of the difference of trading practices in their respective countries. The diversity of interpretation which exists in international contracts has led to many disputes with consequent reference to the Courts. In order to obviate this type of dispute the International Chamber of Commerce introduced in 1936 a set of international rules for the interpretation of trade terms. Incoterms, it was felt, required revision and in 1953 this came about to provide an up-to-date set of rules to bring into line current practice in international trade.

The major difficulties met fall into three categories:

(a) Uncertainty as to the law of what country will be applicable to the contracts;

(b) the difficulties which arise from diversity of interpretation;

(c) the difficulties which arise from inadequate information.

The main aims of the "Incoterms 1953" are to define the liabilities of the parties as clearly and precisely as possible. Where there are major differences in current practice, the principle has been adopted that a contract price settled on the basis of "Incoterms 1953" will provide for minimum liabilities on the part of the seller, leaving it to the parties to provide in their contracts for greater liabilities than there are in the rules, if they wish to do so.

C.I.F. (cost, insurance, freight)

Under this type of contract the seller undertakes to sell the goods at a price which includes all charges including freight and insurance. The respective responsibilities are as follows:—

(A) *The seller must:—*

1. Supply the goods in accordance with the contract of sale, together with evidence of conformity as may be required by the contract.

2. Contract on the usual terms at his own expense for the carriage of the goods to the agreed port of destination by the usual route.

3. Pay freight charges.

4. Pay all transportation charges to the agreed destination.

5. At his own risk and expense obtain any export licence necessary for the export of the goods.

6. Load the goods on board the vessel at his own expense and give due notice to the buyer that the goods have been loaded.

7. Obtain at his own cost in a transferable form a policy of marine insurance against the risks of the carriage.

8. Furnish the buyer without delay a clean bill of lading for the agreed destination, as well as the invoice of the goods shipped and insurance policy. The bill of lading must be in respect of the contract goods. Such bill of lading must be a full set of "shipped" bills of lading.

9. Provide at his own expense the customary packing of the goods.

10. Pay any taxes or dues incurred in respect of the goods up to the time of their loading on board, including any taxes incurred levied because of exportation.

(B) *The buyer must:—*

1. Accept the documents when received from the seller providing they are in conformity with the contract of sale.

2. Receive the goods at the agreed port of destination and pay unloading costs, including lighterage and wharfage charges.

3. Bear all risks of the goods from the time when they shall have effectively passed the ship's rail at the port of shipment.

4. Pay the costs and charges incurred in obtaining the certificate of origin and consular documents.

5. Pay all import Customs duties after discharge, including any rail charges and cartage.

6. Procure and provide at his own risk and expense any import licence or permit which may be required for the importation of the goods.

The above are, broadly speaking, the responsibilities of the respective parties, but local custom may alter certain features.

Prima facie, the property under a c.i.f. contract passes to the buyer on shipment, but it may be passed;

(a) *conditionally*, when the bill of lading is made out in the name of the seller, when it is possible that the property may not pass until the tender of the price—this is often done in exchange for the documents. For example, during the First World War the British Government was held by the Courts to be unable to confiscate a cargo destined to enemy territory because bills of lading had been made out in the sellers' name domiciled in the United States.

(b) *unconditionally*, when the bill of lading is made out in favour of the buyer, or his agent.

Ex works

The seller must:—

1. Supply the goods in conformity with the contract of sale, together with such evidence of conformity as may be required by the contract.

2. Place the goods at the disposal of the buyer at the time as provided in the contract, at the point of delivery named or which is usual for the delivery of such goods and for their loading on the conveyance as provided by the buyer.

3. To provide the packing of such goods as necessary to enable the buyer to take delivery of the goods.

4. Give the buyer reasonable notice as to when the goods will be available.

5. Bear the expense of any checking, measuring, weighing of the goods in order that the goods may be placed at the disposal of the buyer.

6. Bear all other expenses and risks of the goods until they have been placed at the disposal of the buyer.

7. To render every assistance to the buyer in obtaining any documents which are issued in the country of delivery and which the buyer may require for the purpose of exportation and/or importation of the goods.

The buyer must:—

1. Take delivery of the goods as soon as they are placed at his disposal in accordance with the terms of the contract. He must also pay the price of the goods as agreed.

2. Bear all the charges and risks of the goods from the moment they have been placed at his disposal.

3. Pay any Customs duties and taxes that may be levied by reasons of exportation.

4. Where the buyer has reserved to himself a period within which to take delivery of the goods and/or the right to choose the place of delivery and should he fail to give instructions in time, bear the additional costs incurred by this failure and also bear all risks of the goods from the date of the expiration of the period fixed.

5. Pay all the costs of obtaining the various documents required for exportation purposes.

F.A.S. (free alongside ship)

The seller must:—

1. Supply the goods in conformity with the contract of sale, together with such evidence of conformity as may be required by the contract.

2. Deliver the goods alongside the vessel at the loading berth named by the buyer, at the named port of shipment. This must be done in a manner which is customary at the port within the agreed time limits. He must then notify the buyer, without delay, that the goods have been delivered alongside the vessel.

3. Assist the buyer to obtain necessary export licences or other documentation for the export of such goods. This is done at the buyer's expense.

4. Bear all risks and expense of the goods until the cargo has been effectively delivered alongside the vessel, including delivery charges.

5. Provide at his expense necessary packing of the goods.

6. Pay all costs of checking, weighing or measuring of the cargo necessary to effect delivery alongside the vessel.

7. Provide the customary clean document of proof of delivery.

8. Provide the buyer with the certificate of origin, this being paid for by the buyer.

The buyer must:—

1. Give the seller notice of the name, loading berth and the delivery dates to the vessel.

2. Bear all charges and risks of the goods from the time of delivery alongside.

3. Bear any additional costs because the vessel may have failed to arrive on time or shall close for cargo earlier than the stipulated time.

4. Should he fail to name the vessel in time he must bear all additional costs and risks of the cargo because of such failure.

5. Pay all costs of obtaining necessary documentation for the exportation/importation of the goods.

F.O.B. (free on board)

The seller must:—

1. Supply the goods in conformity with the contract of sale, together with such evidence of conformity as may be required by the contract.

2. Deliver the goods on board the vessel named by the buyer at the port of shipment. This must be done within the agreed time and the buyer notified without delay that the goods have been delivered on board.

3. At his own risk and expense obtain any export licence necessary for the export of the goods.

4. Bear all costs and risks of the goods until they have passed ship's rail, including taxes, fees or charges of exportation. He must also pay costs of formalities which he shall have to fulfil in order to load the goods on board.

5. Provide at his expense customary packing of the goods.

6. Pay all costs of necessary checking, weighing or measuring the cargo for purposes of loading on board ship.

7. Provide at his expense customary clean document of proof of delivery of the goods on board.

8. Provide the buyer with the certificate of origin.

9. Render the buyer every assistance in obtaining a bill of lading or other documents issued in the country of shipment which the buyer may require for the importation of the goods into the country of destination.

The buyer must:—

1. At his own expense, charter a vessel or reserve the necessary space on board a vessel and give the seller due notice of the name, loading berth and delivery dates to the vessel.

2. Bear all costs and risks of the goods from the time when they have passed the ship's rail and pay the price provided in the contract.

3. Bear any additional costs incurred because the vessel may have failed to arrive on time, or by the end of the period specified for delivery.

4. Should he fail to name the vessel in time and if he shall have reserved to himself a period within which to take delivery of the goods, should he fail to give detailed instructions in time, bear any additional costs because of such failure.

5. Pay any costs of obtaining a bill of lading.

6. Pay all costs of obtaining documents, including the costs of certificates of origin and consular documents.

CHAPTER 3

CARRIAGE OF GOODS BY SEA ACT 1924
THE HAGUE RULES

In the 19th century there was a great deal of general dissatisfaction with the conditions upon which goods were carried by sea. This unrest came about due to the many elaborate negligence clauses which were introduced into bills of lading.

These clauses were designed completely to defeat the effect of legal decisions, against shipowners, in the Courts. Many such clauses were hopelessly ambiguous and quite impossible to interpret. This in turn led to a ludicrous situation when many shippers, bankers and cargo underwriters were unable to understand the extent of their rights against the carrier.

The liner companies at that time were in a monopolistic position because being relatively few in number they could combine well to agree various terms of carriage, whereas the shippers found they were unable to combine effectively in order to negotiate with the shipowners on equal terms. The general effect of this was for a feeling in the industry of dissatisfaction and growing agitation for governments to introduce legislation to remedy this situation for the protection of shippers, bankers and underwriters.

In 1893 the Harter Act was passed in the United States which laid down many conditions upon which goods were carried by sea. The conditions affected goods being shipped to and from the United States.

This legislation was followed by other governments who introduced similar legislation, namely Australia (the Sea Carriage of Goods Act 1904), Canada (the Water-Carriage of Goods Act 1910) and New Zealand, where a series of new Acts were passed.

In 1921 the Imperial Shipping Committee made recommendations to the British Government that there should be uniform legislation throughout the Empire to standardise the law regarding the carriage of goods by sea.

However, the shipping community favoured the idea of the adoption of a set of uniform rules rather than legislation.

The Maritime Law Committee of the International Law Association therefore held a meeting to discuss the conflicting views of shipowners and cargo interests and did in fact draw up a set of rules known as the Hague Rules 1921. However, the voluntary adoption of the rules did not materialise and there was further agitation for legislation on this issue. This in turn led to the Conference on Maritime Law at Brussels in 1922 where the Hague Rules were adopted as the basis of a draft convention for the unification of certain rules relating to bills of lading.

The International Convention was signed by many participating countries at Brussels on Aug. 25, 1924, and was given force of law in the United Kingdom by the Carriage of Goods by Sea Act 1924.

General features

The general purpose of the Act was to bring about uniformity in regard to the condition of contracts of carriage by sea to which the Act applied. The question, therefore, arose as to what contracts were covered by the Act and, furthermore, to what voyage it applied.

The Act was expressed to apply only to contracts of carriage covered by a bill of lading or similar document of title. Charter-parties are, therefore, outside the scope of the Act, as long as the contract of carriage is so expressed. The moment a bill of lading is issued pursuant to a charter-party, and becomes the contract which regulates the relations of the parties, the Act applied to that bill of lading. So long as it is merely a receipt for the goods shipped, the Act did not apply, because the contract of carriage is the charter-party.

Coasting trade

Owing to strong representations made by parties interested in the coasting trade, the Act allowed such parties freedom of contract so long as the contract is not embodied in a bill of lading, but is contained in a receipt which shall be marked as a non-negotiable document. (The only limitation is that contracts must not be contrary to public policy.)

Live animals

The Act has no application to live animals, and the parties in respect of such shipments are free to contract on any agreed terms.

Deck cargo

Deck cargo is exempt from the conditions of the Act, provided the cargo is expressed in the bill of lading as being carried on deck, and is actually so carried.

Particular goods

Here again, it has been recognised that certain classes of goods, not ordinary commercial shipments made in the ordinary course of trade, should be exempted from the provisions of the Act. The conditions upon which such goods may be carried under any agreed terms are similar to those exempting the coasting trade, namely, that no bill of lading may be issued, and that the agreed terms of carriage are embodied in a receipt marked as non-negotiable.

Voyages covered

Only outward voyages are covered by the Act, that is to say, goods carried from any port in Great Britain or Northern Ireland to any other port whether in or outside Great Britain or Northern Ireland. The conditional exemption of the coasting trade is not affected by this broad definition.

Seaworthiness

Up to the time the Act became law, there was implied in every contract of carriage by sea an absolute warranty that the vessel was seaworthy at the commencement of the voyage, and also at the commencement of each subsequent stage. Only the most clear and unambiguous language in the bill of lading could exclude this implied warranty.

The Act now categorically abolishes the implied warranty of seaworthiness in all contracts to which it applies. The shipowner is still under a legal obligation to exercise due diligence to make the vessel seaworthy in all respects and to make the holds fit for the reception of the cargo, but he is not liable for losses due to unseaworthiness, unless due to want of due diligence on his part.

From loading to discharge

Although the shipowner has certain obligations prior to the loading of the goods on board, the Act leaves him free to contract on any agreed terms in respect of the transit of goods, prior to their loading on board and subsequent to their discharge from the vessel. Before loading and after discharge the rights and obligations of the parties may, in the absence of any special agreement, be controlled by local laws and customs. Only for the period of the voyage are they defined and standardised by the Rules. If the carrier who undertakes the carriage of goods performs additional services (such as those of a forwarding agent), the terms on which such services are rendered must be looked for elsewhere than in the Rules.

Obligation to issue a bill of lading

When goods are delivered to the shipowner he must, on demand, issue to the shipper a bill of lading stating particulars of the goods, and their apparent order or condition. The particulars stated on the bill constitute a *prima facie* case that the goods as therein described have been received into the custody of the carrier. It will be observed that the obligation to issue the bill does not depend upon the goods having been loaded on board the vessel.

The bill of lading which is issued prior to the actual shipment of the goods is a "received for shipment" bill. When the goods are actually loaded, the shipper may demand a "shipped" bill of lading. A "received for shipment" bill of lading may become a "shipped" bill by noting thereon the name of the ship upon which the goods have been loaded and the date of the shipment.

Obligations of the shipper

The shipper must furnish the particulars of the goods to be stated on the bill of lading and the shipper must indemnify the carrier in the event of loss, damage or expense arising or resulting from inaccuracy in such particulars. To make the shipper liable it must be shown that he has been at fault. He is not liable to the carrier for any loss or damage unless the same has been due to "act, fault or neglect of the shipper or his agents or servants".

General Average

The Act expressly provides that the parties may make any reasonable provisions respecting General Average; thus, it has not direct effect upon General Average.

Deviation

Deviation in attempting to save property as well as life is now recognised by the Rules as justifiable, and the carrier will not be liable for loss or damage to cargo so caused. Nor will such deviation or any reasonable deviation be deemed to be a breach of contract. Whether or not a particular deviation is "reasonable" is, in every instance, a question of fact, to be considered in the light of the circumstances prevailing. Unauthorised deviation puts an end to the contract of carriage, and the carrier cannot rely upon the rights and immunities granted in Article IV.

Limitation of liability

Unless the value and nature of the goods are declared and inserted in the bill of lading before the goods are shipped, liability is limited to £100 per package or unit; the parties are, however, free to insert a higher limit, but the shipowner may not restrict his liability to an amount less than this amount. In a case decided in the American Courts, it was held that a limitation of this nature cannot be reduced *pro rata* where the damage to a particular package is partial and not total, and that a clause to this effect in the bill of lading is repugnant to the Rule. The limit of £100 per package is altered, in practice, to £200 in this country by the operation of a gentleman's agreement between British shipowners, P. & I. Associations, merchants and underwriters, which became effective on Aug. 1, 1950, and applies to bills of lading issued on and after Aug. 1, 1949.

Dangerous goods

The provisions in the Act covering dangerous goods are very similar to those contained in the Merchant Shipping Act 1894. If these goods are shipped without the knowledge and assent of the carrier, they may be destroyed or landed, and the shipper must pay any damage caused by such goods. If they have been properly shipped and subsequently become a menace to the ship or cargo, they may also be destroyed and the carrier shall not incur any liability other than an obligation to contribute in General Average (if any).

Notice of loss or damage

The provisions providing for notice of loss or damage to be given are one of the most unsatisfactory features of the Act. Such notice must be given at the time the goods are received into the custody of the receiver or his agent, or, where the damage is not apparent at that time, within three days of delivery of the goods as described in the bill of lading. Notice may be waived in cases where the goods have been the subject of a joint survey at the time of their receipt.

It will be observed that delivery without the required notice only constitutes a *prima facie* case of sound delivery. The consignee may still attempt to show that the loss or damage took place while the goods were in the care of the carrier, but the difficulty of discharging this onus is a heavy one, particularly where there is a transit by craft from the ship to the shore. Even if it is shown that the damage took place before the goods were landed, the consignee cannot recover where the shipowner has exempted himself from liability while the goods are in lighter or craft, as the Act allows him to do, unless the consignee can further show that the loss or damage arose while the goods were on board the ship, and from a cause for which the shipowner was not exempt. Thus, it will be appreciated that, where the onus is upon the consignee to establish his case against the shipowner, the difficulties of so doing are rendered very much greater by the provisions requiring notice to be given.

Exemptions from liability

The broad intention of these exemptions is to free the carrier from navigational risks, which, being insurable, are thrown upon the shipper or owner of the goods.

The details of these exemptions will be considered when the terms of the Act are analysed. In general terms it may be affirmed that the carrier can only be held liable for loss or damage arising from the fault or neglect of the carrier or his servants or agents.

Time limit for bringing suit

The carrier is discharged from all liability for loss or damage unless suit is brought within one year from the time the goods are delivered or should have been delivered. In practice, British shipowners will extend the statutory period for bringing suit for a further 12 months on request, providing there has been no undue delay in making claim. This is a provision of the gentleman's agreement between the British shipowners and other parties which became effective on Aug. 1, 1950.

Benefit of insurance clause

In the past it has been a common thing for shipowners to provide in their bills of lading for the benefit of any insurance effected by the owner of the goods. In effect, whenever the loss was covered by insurance, the shipowners escaped liability, even though they were liable in the first place for the loss or damage. Instead of the insurers being subrogated to the assured's rights against the carrier, the carrier could claim the benefit of the insurance as an assignee.

Bulk cargoes

It has already been stated that, according to the Act, the bill of lading must contain particulars of the goods or cargo carried. Among the required particulars the quantity or weight must be stated, and a *prima facie* case is thus established that the quantity or weight is as described.

There are, however, certain kinds of bulk cargo of which it is practically impossible for either the shipper or the shipowner to check the weight. It would cast a heavy burden upon both parties, unless these cases were provided for. The Act, therefore, provides that where the weight of any bulk cargo is ascertained or accepted by a third party (other than the carrier or shipper) and the fact that the weight has been so ascertained or accepted is stated in the bill of lading, it will not be deemed to constitute a *prima facie* case of the correctness of the weight against either the carrier or the shipper.

RULES RELATING TO BILLS OF LADING

Article I—Definitions

In these Rules the following expressions have the meanings hereby assigned to them respectively, that is to say:—

(a) "Carrier" includes the owner or the charterer who enters into a contract of carriage with a shipper.

(b) "Contract of carriage" applies only to contracts of carriage covered by a bill of lading or any similar document of title, in so far as such document relates to the carriage of goods by sea, including any bill of lading or similar document as aforesaid issued under or pursuant to a charter-party from the moment at which such bill of lading or similar document of title regulates the relations between a carrier and a holder of the same.

(c) "Goods" includes goods, wares, merchandise, and articles of every kind whatsoever except live animals and cargo which by the contract of carriage is stated as being carried on deck and is so carried.

(d) "Ship" means any vessel used for the carriage of goods by sea.

(e) "Carriage of goods" covers the period from the time when the goods are loaded on to the time when they are discharged from the ship.

Article II—Risks

Subject to the provisions of Article VI, under every contract of carriage of goods by sea, the carrier, in relation to the loading, handling, stowage, carriage, custody, care and discharge of such goods, shall be subject to the responsibilities and liabilities and entitled to the rights and immunities hereinafter set forth.

Article III—Duties

1. The carrier shall be bound, before and at the beginning of the voyage, to exercise due diligence to:—

(a) Make the ship seaworthy;

(b) Properly man, equip and supply the ship;

(c) Make the holds, refrigerating and cool chambers, and all other parts of the ship in which goods are carried, fit and safe for their reception, carriage and preservation.

2. Subject to the provisions of Article IV, the carrier shall properly and carefully load, handle, stow, carry, keep, care for, and discharge the goods carried.

3. After receiving the goods into his charge the carrier or the master or agent of the carrier shall on demand of the shipper issue to the shipper a bill of lading showing among other things;

(a) The loading marks necessary for identification of the goods are the same as furnished in writing by the shipper before the loading of such goods starts, provided such marks are stamped or otherwise shown clearly upon the goods if uncovered, or on the cases or coverings in which such goods are contained, in such a manner as should ordinarily remain legible until the end of the voyage;

(b) Either the number of packages or pieces, or the quantity or weight, as the case may be, as furnished in writing by the shipper;

(c) The apparent order and condition of the goods;

Provided that no carrier, master or agent of the carrier shall be bound to state or show in the bill of lading any marks, number, quantity, or weight which he has reasonable ground for suspecting not accurately to represent the goods actually received, or which he has had no reasonable means of checking.

4. Such a bill of lading shall be *prima facie* evidence of the receipt by the carrier of the goods as therein described in accordance with paragraph 3(a), (b) and (c).

5. The shipper shall be deemed to have guaranteed to the carrier the accuracy at the time of shipment of the marks, number, quantity, and weight as furnished by him, and the shipper shall indemnify the carrier against all loss, damages and expenses arising or resulting from inaccuracies in such particulars. The right of the carrier to such indemnity shall in no way limit his responsibility and liability under the contract of carriage to any person other than the shipper.

6. Unless notice of loss or damage and the general nature of such loss or damage be given in writing to the carrier or his agent at the port of discharge before or at the time of the removal of the goods into the custody of the person entitled to delivery thereof under the contract of carriage, or, if the loss or damage be not apparent, within three days, such removal shall be *prima facie* evidence of the delivery by the carrier of the goods as described in the bill of lading.

The notice in writing need not be given if the state of the goods has at the time of their receipt been the subject of joint survey or inspection.

In any event the carrier and the ship shall be discharged from all liability in respect of loss or damage unless suit is brought within one year after delivery of the goods or the date when the goods should have been delivered.

In the case of any actual or apprehended loss or damage, the carrier and the receiver shall give all reasonable facilities to each other for inspecting and tallying the goods.

7. After the goods are loaded the bill of lading to be issued by the carrier, master or agent of the carrier, to the shipper shall, if the shipper so demands, be a "shipped" bill of lading, provided that if the shipper shall have previously taken up any document

of title to such goods, he shall surrender the same as against the issue of a "shipped" bill of lading, but at the option of the carrier such document of title may be noted at the port of shipment by the carrier, master or agent with the name or names of the ship or ships upon which the goods have been shipped, and the date or dates of shipment, and when so noted the same shall for the purpose of this Article be deemed to constitute a "shipped" bill of lading.

8. Any clause, covenant or agreement in a contract of carriage relieving the carrier or ship from liability for loss or damage to or in connection with goods arising from negligence, fault or failure in the duties and obligations provided in this Article or lessening such liability otherwise than as provided in these Rules shall be null and void and of no effect.

A benefit of insurance or similar clause shall be deemed to be a clause relieving the carrier from liability.

Article IV—Rights and Immunities

1. Neither the carrier nor the ship shall be liable for loss or damage arising or resulting from unseaworthiness unless caused by want of due diligence on the part of the carrier to make the ship seaworthy and to secure that the ship is properly manned, equipped and supplied, and to make the holds, refrigerating and cool chambers and all other parts of the ship in which goods are carried fit and safe for their reception, carriage and preservation in accordance with the provisions of para. I of Article III. Whenever loss or damage has resulted from unseaworthiness the burden of proving the exercise of due diligence shall be on the carrier or other person claiming exemption under this section.

2. Neither the carrier nor the ship shall be responsible for loss or damage arising or resulting from:

    (a) Act, neglect, or default of the master, mariner, pilot, or the servant of the carrier in the navigation or in the management of the ship;

    (b) Fire, unless caused by the actual fault or privity of the carrier;

    (c) Perils, dangers and accidents of the sea or other navigable waters;

    (d) Act of God;

    (e) Act of war;

    (f) Act of public enemies;

    (g) Arrest or restraint of princes, rulers or people, or seizure under legal process;

    (h) Quarantine restrictions;

(i) Act or omission of the shipper or owner of the goods, his agent or representative;

(j) Strikes, or lock-outs or stoppage or restraint of labour from whatever cause, whether partial or general;

(k) Riots and civil commotions;

(l) Saving or attempting to save life or property at sea;

(m) Wastage in bulk or weight or any other loss or damage arising from inherent defect, quality, or vice of the goods;

(n) Insufficiency of packing;

(o) Insufficiency or inadequacy of marks;

(p) Latent defects not discoverable by due diligence;

(q) Any other cause arising without the actual fault or privity of the carrier, or without the fault or neglect of the agents or servants of the carrier, but the burden of proof shall be on the person claiming the benefit of this exception to shew that neither the actual fault or neglect of the agents or servants of the carrier contributed to the loss or damage.

3. The shipper shall not be responsible for loss or damage sustained by the carrier or the ship arising or resulting from any cause without the act, fault or neglect of the shipper, his agents or his servants.

4. Any deviation in saving or attempting to save life or property at sea or any reasonable deviation shall not be deemed to be an infringement or breach of these Rules or of the contract of carriage, and the carrier shall not be liable for any loss or damage resulting therefrom.

5. Neither the carrier nor the ship shall in any event be or become liable for any loss or damage to or in connection with goods in an amount exceeding £100 per package, or unit, or the equivalent of that sum in other currency, unless the nature and value of such goods have been declared by the shipper before shipment and inserted in the bill of lading. This declaration if embodied in the bill of lading shall be *prima facie* evidence, but shall not be binding or conclusive on the carrier. By agreement between the carrier, master or agent of the carrier and the shipper, another maximum amount than that mentioned in this paragraph may be fixed, provided that such maximum shall not be less than the figure above named. Neither the carrier nor the ship shall be responsible in any event for loss or damage to or in connection with goods if the nature or value thereof has been knowingly mis-stated by the shipper in the bill of lading.

6. Goods of an inflammable, explosive or dangerous nature to the shipment whereof the carrier, master or agent of the carrier has not consented with knowledge of their nature and character, may at any time before discharge be landed at any place or destroyed or rendered innocuous by the carrier without compensation, and the shipper of such goods shall be liable for all damages and expenses directly or indirectly arising out of or resulting from such shipment. If any such goods shipped with such knowledge and consent shall become a danger to the ship or cargo, they may in like manner be landed at any place or destroyed or rendered innocuous by the carrier without liability on the part of the carrier except to general average, if any.

Article V—Surrender of Rights and Immunities and increase of Responsibilities and Liabilities

A carrier shall be at liberty to surrender in whole or in part all or any of his rights and immunities or to increase any of his responsibilities and liabilities under the Rules contained in any of these Articles, provided such surrender or increase shall be embodied in the bill of lading issued to the shipper. The provisions of these Rules shall not be applicable to charter-parties, but if bills of lading are issued in the case of a ship under a charter-party they shall comply with the terms of these Rules. Nothing in these Rules shall be held to prevent the insertion in a bill of lading of any lawful provision regarding general average.

Article VI—Special Conditions

Notwithstanding the provisions of the preceding Articles, a carrier, master or agent of the carrier, and a shipper shall in regard to any particular goods be at liberty to enter into any agreement in any terms as to the responsibility and liability of the carrier for such goods, and as to the rights and immunities of the carrier in respect of such goods, or his obligation as to seaworthiness, so far as this stipulation is not contrary to public policy, or the care or diligence of his servants or agents in regard to the loading, handling, stowage, carriage, custody, care and discharge of the goods carried by sea, provided that in this case no bill of lading has been or shall be issued and that the terms agreed shall be embodied in a receipt which shall be a non-negotiable document and shall be marked as such. Any agreement so entered into shall have full legal effect.

Provided that this Article shall not apply to ordinary commercial shipments made in the ordinary course of trade, but only to other shipments where the character or condition of the property to be carried, or the circumstances, terms and conditions under which the carriage is to be performed, are such as reasonably to justify a special agreement.

Article VII—Limitations on the Application of the Rules

Nothing herein contained shall prevent a carrier or a shipper from entering into any agreement, stipulation, condition, reservation or exemption as to the responsibility and liability of the carrier or the ship for the loss or damage to or in connection with the custody and care and handling of goods prior to the loading on and subsequent to the discharge from the ship on which the goods are carried by sea.

Article VIII—Limitation of Liability

The provisions of these Rules shall not affect the rights and obligations of the carrier under any statute for the time being in force relating to the limitation of the liability of owners of seagoing vessels.

Article IX—Monetary Units

The monetary units mentioned in these Rules are to be taken to be gold value.

CHAPTER 4

CARRIAGE OF GOODS BY SEA ACT 1971
THE HAGUE-VISBY RULES

The original Hague Rules as embodied in the Carriage of Goods by Sea Act 1924 have now been modified and extended to a certain extent. This has meant that the 1924 Act has now been repealed and replaced by the Carriage of Goods by Sea Act 1971.

This Act received the Royal Assent on Apr. 8, 1971, and fully incorporates the amendments made to the Hague Rules of 1924 by the Brussels Protocol of 1968.

Sufficient countries have ratified the Protocol and the new rules came into force in the United Kingdom on June 23, 1977.

The ratifying or acceding countries are as follows:—

France	Belgium	Ecuador
Denmark	Poland	Lebanon
Norway	Tonga	Singapore
Sweden	German Democratic Republic	Syria
Switzerland		
United Kingdom		

It is apparent that the number of contracting States has increased and it is understood that a number of other countries intend ratifying the Protocol. The following States have now been added:—Bermuda, Hong Kong, Gibraltar, Isle of Man, The Netherlands, Sri Lanka, Spain (not yet in force).

The Protocol applies to every bill of lading relating to the carriage of goods between ports in two different States, whether or not there is a clause paramount incorporating the Hague-Visby Rules providing:—

(a) The bill of lading is issued in a contracting State, or

(b) The carriage is from a port in a contracting State, or

(c) The contract contained in or evidenced by the bill of lading provides that the rules or the legislation of any State giving effect to them are to govern the contract, whatever may be the nationality of the ship, the carrier, the shipper, the consignee, or any other interested person.

The Carriage of Goods by Sea Act 1971 came into force on June 23, 1977, and it is further understood that the Carriage of Goods by Sea Act 1924 continued to apply to bills of lading issued before June 23 and to bills of lading issued on or after June 23, but before Dec. 23, 1977, if they were issued pursuant to contracts entered into before June 23.

The following are the main alterations to the Hague Rules made by the Brussels Protocol and reflected in the Carriage of Goods by Sea Act 1971:

1. Article 3, para. 4 of the Rules has been amended to the effect that statements in bills of lading shall be regarded as *conclusive evidence* when such bills of lading have been transferred to a third party acting in good faith.

2. Article 3, para. 6, the third sub-paragraph is amended to provide that in any event there shall be no liability in respect of goods unless suit is brought within one year, it being permissible to extend such period should the parties so agree.

3. A new paragraph has been added to Article 3 (para. 6 Bis) so that recourse actions may be brought after the expiration of the one-year time limit, within the time limit allowed by the law of the Court seized of the case.

4. Article 4, para. 5 has been amended in its entirety regarding limitation of liability and the amendments cover the following main points:

    (a) Weight (kilo) is an alternative to package or unit as a basis for limitation and the basis giving the higher figure shall be adopted.

    (b) The previous per package or unit limitation of £100 has been raised to Poincaré francs 10,000 and the limit of liability per kilo is Poincaré francs 30.

    (c) The total amount recoverable in respect of a claim is to be calculated by reference to the value of goods at the place and time at which the goods are discharged from the ship.

    (d) Where a container, pallet or similar article of transport is used to consolidate the goods the question as to whether limitation is based on per package or unit, or on weight, is decided by referring to the bill of lading itself. If packages or units are enumerated in the bill of lading as being packed in the container, then the unit basis will be adopted, otherwise the container itself will be the basis.

5. A completely new Article 4 (Bis) "Himalaya Clause" has been added to the Rules in order that servants and agents of the carrier will be entitled to benefit from the definitions and limits of liability at present agreed to carriers. Servants or agents shall not be entitled to avail themselves of these provisions if it is proved that the damage resulted from an act or omission of the servant, or agent, done with intent to cause damage, or with knowledge that damage will probably result.

One of the major changes brought about by the introduction of the Hague-Visby Rules is the "Container Rule".

The container revolution has necessitated amendments in the law for the carriage of goods by sea.

The Hague-Visby provides rules to enable a decision to be made as to whether the container should be treated as a single unit for the purposes of limitation of liability in respect of loss or damage. Alternatively, whether the contents of the container, i.e. the number of packages, can be used as separate units for the purposes of limitation.

The decision as to whether the container or the cargo itself can be used to calculate limitation is an extremely important one and there have been no cases before British Courts to decide the issue.

However, in the American Courts, a number of cases have been fought on this issue and the general result has been to favour the unit of cargo inside the container to be used for limitation purposes.

Therefore, the Hague-Visby Rules have amended and brought certainty to this situation and now specifically provides that where a container, pallet, or similar article of transport is used to consolidate goods the number of packages or units enumerated in the bill of lading shall be used when calculating limitation of liability. However, if such contents are not enumerated in the bill of lading then the article of transport, i.e. the container, shall be used for the purposes of limitation.

CHAPTER 5

THE BILLS OF LADING ACT 1855

When making a study of the Hague-Visby Rules as enacted by the Carriage of Goods by Sea Act 1971 it is essential to give consideration to the Bills of Lading Act 1855 and the reasons for its introduction.

Prior to its introduction, under Common Law contracts were not assignable. Therefore, when a bill of lading was passed to a consignee, for example, with the intention of passing the property in the goods, it did not transfer the rights and liabilities under the contract of affreightment to the consignee. The only effect was indeed to pass to the consignee the property in the goods.

The introduction of the Act effected a complete change in the situation which existed at that time which is made abundantly clear from the provisions of the Act:—

> "And whereas it frequently happens that the goods in respect of which bills of lading purport to be signed have not been laden on board, and it is proper that such bills of lading in the hands of a *bona fide* holder for value should not be questioned by the master or other person signing the same on the ground of the goods not having been laden as aforesaid:

> Be it therefore enacted by the Queen's most Excellent Majesty, by and with the Advice and consent of the Lords Spiritual and Temporal, and Commons, in this present Parliament assembled, and by the authority of the same as follows:

> *Section 1*: Every consignee of goods named in a bill of lading, and every endorsee of a bill of lading to whom the property in the goods therein mentioned shall pass, upon or by reason of such consignment or endorsement, shall have transferred to and vested to him all rights to suit, and be subject to the same liabilities in respect of such goods as if the contract contained in the bill of lading had been made with himself.

> *Section 2*: Nothing herein contained shall prejudice or affect any rights of stoppage in transitu, or any right to claim freight against the original shipper or owner, or any liability of the consignee or endorsee by reason or in consequence of his being such consignee or endorsee, or of his receipt of the goods by reason or in consequence of such consignment or endorsement.

> *Section 3*: Every bill of lading in the hands of a consignee or endorsee for valuable consideration representing goods to have been shipped on board a vessel shall be conclusive evidence of such shipment as against the master or other person signing the same, notwithstanding that such goods or some part thereof may not have been so shipped, unless such holder of the bill of lading shall have had actual notice at the time of receiving the same that the goods had not been in fact laden on board. Provided, that the master or other person so signing may

exonerate himself in respect of such misrepresentation by showing that it was caused without any default on his part, and wholly by the fraud of the shipper, or of the holder, or some person under whom the holder claims".

The provisions of section 1 of the Act stipulated that a bill of lading not only became a document of title to the goods in the hands of an endorsee for value, but also passed to such parties the rights and liabilities under the contract. As a result of this legislation the requirements of trade by the Carriage of Goods by Sea were satisfied and consignees, bankers and other parties (who were not effectively party to the original contract with the carrier and had no control over its terms) now had rights in the bill of lading.

Section 2 of the Act provides that nothing in the Act shall prejudice in any way any rights of "stoppage in transitu" or any right to claim freight against the original shipper or owner. The subject of "stoppage in transitu" is dealt with fully under the provisions of the Sale of Goods Act 1979.

However, by way of further observation it may happen that after the goods have been loaded on board a vessel, the master or owner may receive a demand from a third party claiming delivery and his right to the goods.

The cargo has probably been the subject of some special sale contract conditions and whilst in transit from the seller to the buyer it becomes apparent that the buyer is insolvent and is unable to pay for the goods.

In these circumstances the unpaid seller may instruct the master or shipowner not to deliver the goods to the particular purchaser but to return the goods to him. This action is known as "stoppage in transitu" and is available to the seller in accordance with the Sale of Goods Act 1979. The circumstances under which this action may be exercised are fully discussed in the chapter pertaining to the Sale of Goods.

It was the ruling of the Court in the case of *Grant* v. *Norway* 1851 which was the predominant reason for the introduction of section 3 of the Bills of Lading Act.

This case came before the Courts in 1851 and concerned the master of a vessel signing a bill of lading acknowledging the receipt and shipment of 12 bales of silk in apparent good order and condition. It was a fact that this consignment was never shipped.

It was apparent that the merchant to whom the bill of lading was issued endorsed the bill to the claimants in these proceedings as security for a debt. The debt remained unsettled and then proceedings were commenced against the shipowner. The proceedings were dismissed by the Court on the grounds that the master's authority extended only to acts which are usual to the normal ship operation. It was considered that it was not usual for a master to sign bills of lading for goods that were not shipped on board. The Court ruled that the master had no authority from the shipowner to sign the bill of lading for the goods which were not shipped and his signature did not in any way bind the shipowner. As a result of this case therefore section 3 of the Act was introduced.

It is, however, extremely important to emphasise the position, as related to section 3 of the Act, with the rule of estoppel with regard to the condition of the goods. If the bill of lading, which acknowledges receipt of the goods, has upon it a remark or clause showing the condition of the goods, the carrier is estopped from showing that the goods were not in apparent good order and condition as in the bill of lading.

CHAPTER 6

THE PRINCIPLES AND PRACTICE OF GENERAL AVERAGE

An Introduction to General Average

The origins of General Average are most ancient but the general principles were first formulated by the Ancient Greeks when dealing with problems relating to jettison. However, as the doctrine of General Average developed, various other types of losses were added to jettison. The most important aspect being that the expenditure of money was recognised as being in principle no different from the sacrifice of part of the property, if it was incurred in the same circumstances.

General Average developed to varying degrees over the centuries in the leading of years before shipowners and merchants even considered the idea of protecting themselves from the financial risks involved in marine commerce by means of insurance.

It must be emphasised at this point that General Average exists and must be considered entirely separately from Marine Insurance. It is essential to the understanding of the practice and principles of General Average that Marine Insurance considerations be ignored, in the first instance.

General Average developed to varying degrees over the centuries in the leading maritime countries and by the late 19th century there were in existence throughout the world substantial differences in law and practice. In view of the international nature of shipping the situation which had developed was obviously unsuitable. Various attempts were made to obtain uniformity on an international basis and this resulted in the adoption of the York-Antwerp Rules.

York-Antwerp Rules

These rules laid down specific rules and statements of the general principles relating to General Average and its adjustment. The earliest version of the rules was confined to the clarification of various matters on which practice in many countries differed.

For all practical purposes it may be assumed that when General Average arises on ocean-going vessels, under modern commercial conditions, the York-Antwerp Rules will apply. The latest version of the rules, York-Antwerp Rules 1974, has improved and simplified to some extent the application of the rules of General Average but by its very nature makes the correct interpretation a very specialised task. It therefore follows that for all practical purposes it may be assumed that when a General Average situation occurs on a vessel under modern commercial conditions the York-Antwerp Rules will apply.

Principles of General Average

Firstly, the term "General Average". You will probably be aware the word "Average" in its maritime sense has nothing to do with its ordinary everyday meaning. It is derived from the old Latin words "avere" which meant property and the later Latin word "averia" which came to mean a charge upon or loss of property. For centuries now "Average" has been used as a comprehensive word to describe a partial loss, damage or expenses arising from a maritime accident.

The word "General" simply means all average loss, damages which are general, or common, to all the principal parties to the joint venture of the voyage, i.e. to the owners of the ship, freight and cargo, the burden of which has to be shared by them all.

To get to the root principles of General Average we must look at the definition given under the York-Antwerp Rules:

> "There is a General Average act when, and only when, any extraordinary sacrifice or expenditure is intentionally and reasonably made or incurred for the common safety for the purpose of preserving from peril the property involved in a common maritime adventure".

The definition may be segregated into four essential features:

(a) *The sacrifice or expenditure must be extraordinary:—*

thus ordinary expenses incurred or losses suffered by the shipowner in fulfilment of his contract of affreightment are not admitted as General Average.

The application of this principle can be best demonstrated by the example of damage caused to the machinery or boilers of a ship which has gone ashore and is in a position of peril and in endeavouring to refloat sustains this damage. The damage shall be allowed in General Average when shown to have arisen from an actual intention to refloat the ship for the common safety at the risk of such damage occurring.

Working the engines of a ship ashore is considered to be an abuse of the machinery and therefore extraordinary. The working of a ship's engines whilst afloat, however much the adventure may have been in peril, is considered as part of the normal function of the machinery and any resultant damage is not admitted as General Average.

(b) *The act must be intentional and voluntary:—*

the General Average act must in no way be inevitable and it should be stressed that the property cannot in reality be said to have been "sacrificed" if it in fact was already lost at the time of the so-called sacrifice. This principle may best be shown by the example of a loss or damage sustained by cutting away wreck or parts of the ship which have been previously damaged or effectively lost by accident. This shall not be made good in General Average.

(c) *There must be peril:*—

the peril need not be of an imminent nature but it must be real and substantial. There is a very fine dividing line between action taken for the common safety in a time of peril which may best be illustrated by the following example:

A vessel adrift in mid-ocean without operative engines would be in a position of peril even if the weather was calm and at no immediate risk of suffering further loss or damage, whereas, if a master were quite prudently to seek shelter for a sound vessel in an anchorage, having received reports of an approaching storm, this would not be regarded as giving rise to a General Average situation.

(d) *Common safety:*—

the action must be taken for the "common safety" and not merely for the safety of part of the property involved in the venture.

As an example to illustrate this facet, suppose a vessel was carrying (as part of her cargo) refrigerated cargo and the refrigerating machinery broke down whilst the vessel was on her voyage through the tropics, making it absolutely imperative for her to put into port to effect repairs. In such a case as this any threat of loss or damage would be limited to the refrigerated cargo and, so far as the ship and remaining cargo was concerned, the voyage could continue safely. The deviation to the port of repair would not in these circumstances be General Average.

Examples of General Average

The following are a number of examples of casualties which frequently give rise to General Average and of the types of General Average sacrifices and expenditure which are likely to be involved:

Stranding

Damage to vessel and machinery through efforts to refloat.
Loss of or damage to cargo through jettison or forced discharge.
Cost of discharging, storing and reloading any cargo so discharged.
Port of refuge expenses.

Fire

Damage to ship or cargo due to efforts to extinguish the fire.
Port of refuge expenses.

Shortage of Bunkers
> Loss of ship's materials or cargo burnt as fuel.
> Port of refuge expenses.

Shifting of Cargo in Heavy Weather
> Jettison.
> Port of refuge expenses.

In addition to the sacrifices and expenditures mentioned above any of these occurrences could give rise to a claim for salvage services. Salvage services, strictly, fall in a separate category as distinct from General Average, but Rule VI of the York-Antwerp Rules 1974 provides that any payments made in that respect should be treated as General Average.

THE PRACTICE OF GENERAL AVERAGE

The obligation to contribute to General Average is not derived from any Contract of Affreightment but arises from the general maritime law irrespective of any such contract. However, the parties may make special provision in the contract regarding General Average, the most common being a clause to the effect that General Average is to be adjusted in accordance with the York-Antwerp Rules. Such stipulations may be contained in the charter-party or in the bills of lading.

Usually it is the shipowner who is primarily concerned to see that rights in General Average are protected since it is usually he who is called upon to pay the General Average expenses. The shipowner has a lien on the cargo whilst in his custody for its contribution to General Average, which gives him the right to demand payment of that contribution as a condition of delivery of the goods. In practice, however, the amount of the contribution can never be assessed at that time and the lien is therefore used to enforce the giving of satisfactory security instead of payment. This usually consists of the signature by the parties to Lloyd's Form of Average Bond, together with (when warranted by the amounts involved) payment by the cargo owner of a cash deposit or provision of a satisfactory guarantee, usually by underwriters, instead of a deposit.

General Average "Declaration"

Whenever a General Average act takes place General Average exists, whether it is declared or not. There are a few countries where it is necessary to make a formal declaration of General Average but the local agents should be aware of the local requirements and should advise shipowners accordingly. In the majority of cases the so-called declaration of General Average is merely a decision by the shipowner to collect General Average security from the concerned in cargo.

General Average security

The form of General Average security required will be decided by the shipowners following full consultation with the average adjusters and, when time permits, full detailed instructions will be sent to the shipowners' agents at the ports of discharge. Security will normally be required in one of the following ways:—

(a) By obtaining cargo consignee's signature to the Lloyd's Form of Average Bond. This procedure is used where the amount involved is small.

(b) By obtaining signed Lloyd's Form of Average Bond together with payment of a cash deposit or provision of a satisfactory guarantee by a reputable underwriter in lieu of such deposit.

(c) In cases of extreme urgency, when the approximate amount of General Average cannot be assessed in time, by cargo consignee's signature to Lloyd's Form of Average Bond, with the following additional clause:

"The Parties of the second part also undertake to pay a cash deposit on account of General Average, if called upon to do so, when the approximate amount of General Average is known."

Average Bonds

In the normal course of events following a General Average occurrence, special printed forms of Average Bond are sent to the ports of destination by the shipowners or the average adjusters. There is also in existence a standard Lloyd's Form of Average Bond which is available from Lloyd's agents.

It is important that all the details provided for in the schedule to the form should be clearly shown to avoid confusion and further enquiries in the future. In particular, the full name and address of the consignee's firm and not merely the name of the individual signing the Bond is required.

It is also essential to detail the precise quantity of the goods to be included, supported by details of bills of lading and ports of destination.

Underwriters' guarantees

It is extremely common in these days for shipowners to accept underwriters' guarantees instead of requiring cash deposits. This practice, of course, has many advantages, especially a considerable saving in administrative costs.

It is important to emphasise that the provision of a guarantee is in no way an alternative to the consignee's signature to an Average Bond. Both the Average Bond and guarantee must be signed before the goods in question can be released.

LLOYD'S AVERAGE BOND.

LAB 77

BURDON & CLARK
Average Adjusters
1 CHURCH ENTRY
LONDON, EC4V 5EU

To ....

Owner(s) of the ....

Voyage and date ....

       Port of shipment ....

       Port of destination/discharge ....

       Bill of lading or waybill number(s) ....

Quantity and description of goods

In consideration of the delivery to us or to our order, on payment of the freight due, of the goods noted above we agree to pay the proper proportion of any salvage and/or general average and/or special charges which may hereafter be ascertained to be due from the goods or the shippers or owners thereof under an adjustment prepared in accordance with the provisions of the contract of affreightment governing the carriage of the goods or, failing any such provision, in accordance with the law and practice of the place where the common maritime adventure ended and which is payable in respect of the goods by the shippers or owners thereof.

We also agree to:

(i) furnish particulars of the value of the goods, supported by a copy of the commercial invoice rendered to us or, if there is no such invoice, details of the shipped value and

(ii) make a payment on account of such sum as is duly certified by the average adjusters to be due from the goods and which is payable in respect of the goods by the shippers or owners thereof.

Date   Signature of receiver of goods

Full name and address

VALUATION FORM

To ....

Owner(s) of the ....

Voyage and date ....

     Port of shipment ....

     Port of destination/discharge ....

     Bill of lading or waybill number(s) ....

Quantity and description of goods	Particulars of value	
	A Invoice value	**B** Shipped value (specify currency)
Currency		

1. If the goods are insured please state the following details (if known):—

    Name and address of insurers or brokers ....

    Policy or certificate number and date ....   Insured value ....

2. If the goods arrived subject to loss or damage, please state nature and extent thereof ....

    ....

    and ensure that copies of supporting documents are forwarded either direct or through the insurers to the average adjusters named below.

3. If a general average deposit has been paid, please state:—

      (a) Amount of the deposit ....   (b) Deposit receipt number ....

      (c) Whether you have made any claim on your insurers

        for reimbursement ....

Date ....   Signature ....

Full name and address ....

....

NOTES

1. If the goods form the subject of a commercial transaction, fill in column A with the amount of the commercial invoice rendered to you, **and attach a copy of this invoice hereto.**

2. If there is no commercial invoice covering the goods, state the shipped value, if known to you, in column B.

3. In either case, state the currency involved.

4. The shipowners have appointed as average adjusters ....

    to whom this form should be sent duly completed together with a copy of the commercial invoice.

BURDON & CLARK
Average Adjusters
1 CHURCH ENTRY
LONDON, EC4V 5EU

TELEGRAPHIC ADDRESS:
"DENOTEMENT, LONDON, E.C.4."

TELEPHONE: 01 - 236 7662/3

TELEX: 896691 TLXIR G
(PREFIX "ADJUSTERS")

BURDON & CLARK

AVERAGE ADJUSTERS

1, CHURCH ENTRY,
LONDON, EC4V 5EU

AND AT
NEWCASTLE UPON TYNE

CARGO UNDERWRITERS' GUARANTEE TO THE SHIPOWNERS

In consideration of the delivery of the undermentioned cargo to the Consignees thereof without the requirement of a deposit, we, the undersigned, being Underwriters on the said merchandise, hereby guarantee the payment to the Shipowners of the contribution for General Average and/or Salvage and/or Particular and/or other charges which may hereafter be ascertained to be due in respect of the said cargo, and to make prompt payments on account thereof upon Burdon & Clark's certificate.

VESSEL:

VOYAGE:

ACCIDENT:

CARGO: (i.e. B/L No., Marks & Description)

SIGNATURE: (further cargo details may
                                                   be inserted overleaf)

DATE:

NAME & ADDRESS OF
COMPANY SIGNING:

UNDERWRITERS' REFERENCE
(Claim No. or Policy No., etc.)

NOTE FOR DEPOSITORS: IF INSURED you may wish to send this receipt together with the original policy or certificate of insurance to your insurers who, subject to the policy conditions, may be prepared to refund this deposit. IF NOT INSURED you should notify the Average Adjusters direct of your interest and retain this receipt until the adjustment is issued when any credit balance can be claimed.

NOTE FOR INSURERS: When a repayment of this deposit has been made, advise the Average Adjusters and thus assist in final settlement.

NO DUPLICATE OF THIS RECEIPT CAN BE ISSUED.

No. ....

GENERAL AVERAGE DEPOSIT RECEIPT.

LLOYD'S FORM.

Dated at .... 19 ......

Vessel .... from .... to ....

Nature and date of Accident ....

RECEIVED from Messrs. ....

the sum of ....

deposit on account of General Average and or Salvage and or Charges,

being .... per cent on ....

provisionally adopted as the contributory value of the following goods, viz.:

Marks and Nos. and Description of Interest to be inserted here.

B/L or Waybill No ....

for and on behalf of the Trustee(s) or nominated representative(s).

N.B.—The refund, if any, will be made only to the bearer of, and in exchange for, this Receipt, and will be the whole balance of the deposit after satisfying the General Average and or Salvage and or Charges, without deduction or set off of any other claims of the Shipowner against the Shipper or Consignee.

BURDON & CLARK

The General Average will be adjusted in ....

Average Adjusters and the Shipowners have given the

necessary instructions to Messrs. .... Average Adjusters

1 CHURCH ENTRY

LONDON, EC4V 5EU

No. ....

General Average Deposit Receipt.

LLOYD'S FORM.

Dated at ....

.... 19 ......

Vessel ....

Depositors, Messrs. ....

Contributory Value (provisional) ....

B/L or Waybill No. ....

Amount of Deposit ....

Description of Goods:

14-1-68 wf-25

It is a frequent occurrence that guarantees are provided in a country other than that where the Average Bond is obtained. Since the cargo cannot be released until both documents have been signed this will necessitate collation of information by the ship's agent who has control of the release of the goods.

Cash deposits

The rate of deposit to be collected by the shipowner in a General Average situation will be advised as a percentage on the arrived value of the cargo at destination, normally based upon the invoice values. Where it may be found that the goods are damaged and the agents are not satisfied that an accurate assessment of the damage can be made at the time, the General Average deposit should be collected on the full value of the goods and the consignee advised to apply for a partial refund at a later time.

The Lloyd's Form of Deposit Receipt should be used in all cases. A separate deposit receipt should be issued for each individual shipment or consignment and the counterfoils to the receipts should be accurately completed and kept to be submitted eventually to the average adjusters.

General Average adjustment and settlement

The adjustment of General Average is undertaken by average adjusters who are employed by the shipowner to prepare a complete statement detailing the full circumstances of the occurrence, together with all expenditure incurred. They will apportion these costs between the interested parties, i.e. shipowners, cargo interests, freight and/or hire.

To prepare this complex statement the adjuster will require all General Average security documents including Average Bonds, Average Guarantees and Cash Deposit Receipts.

Many further documents are required, all casualty reports, log extracts, protests, survey reports, cables and other evidence relating to port of refuge operations.

In this connection it is extremely important to retain all accounts for disbursements incurred, complete with supporting vouchers. A special note should also be kept at the time of the occurrence to reflect any circumstances which have arisen which may necessitate possible division of such disbursements at a later time.

Cargo values

Prior to the adoption of the York-Antwerp Rules 1974, it was usually necessary to submit to the receivers of the cargo a valuation form for completion and signature by them before the contributory value of the goods could be calculated. Under the 1974 Rules this should be unnecessary and, in the majority of cases, all that will be required will be attachment of a copy invoice to the Average Bond.

General Average settlement

Following completion of the General Average adjustment copies will be sent to the agents at ports where settlements are to be effected giving full particulars and instructions. It should be emphasised that frequently documents of title, including original deposit receipts, will be required before settlement can be effected. It may be in certain circumstances, should these documents have been mislaid, that the average adjuster would recommend settlement against an appropriate letter of indemnity.

General Average (Vessels in Ballast)

The foregoing remarks have assumed that the vessel had cargo on board at the time of the casualty. General Average can, however, arise whenever property of different owners is involved in one, common, marine adventure. In the case of a vessel with no cargo on board, the vessel herself, the fuel bunkers on board, hired radio equipment and other items of equipment or stores would be compelled to contribute to the General Average.

General Average settlements as between shipowners, charterers and owners of radio equipment and between the underwriters concerned involve no need for General Average security or similar formalities.

CHAPTER 7

THE ROLE OF THE PROTECTION AND INDEMNITY CLUBS

It is an extremely difficult task to place the role of the P. & I. Clubs in the many areas of shipping but it is true to state that maritime trade could not exist without marine insurance. Neither shipowners nor cargo owners would venture on to the high seas with their property without adequate insurance protection. Today a shipowner has to be as prompt to protect himself in a P. & I. Club against his liabilities as he is to protect himself against the loss of his ships.

In the London market there are Lloyd's underwriters, the insurance companies and the mutual clubs. Lloyd's and the companies insure the ships and their cargoes and the mutual P. & I. Clubs insure the shipowners' liabilities.

P. & I. risks are in general about shipowners' liabilities. A shipowner faces a long list of potential liabilities, some are tortious, based on negligence, some arise out of contracts under which the shipowner assumes responsibility for agreed categories of loss or damage, and some are imposed by statute law or by official regulations. The claims which the shipowner faces, and which the shipbroker or agent may be called upon to assist, are endlessly varied in size and kind, ranging from a cargo claim for the shortage of a case of apples to a claim for damage to a dock costing millions of dollars. He may be liable to persons injured on board his ships, or for damage to port installations, or for damage to other ships in collisions, or for cargo damage, and so the list is endless.

P. & I. insurance is very flexible; it is constantly changing as the years go by to fall into line with the changing laws of various countries throughout the world. It is a self-governing market, in which the assured (the shipowners) say what cover they want, and if possible it is given to them without any government or other intervention or control. Each club is in fact entirely controlled by the members, who are simply the insured shipowners.

A P. & I. Club is controlled by the members themselves through a board of directors elected by themselves. The directors deal with policy matters and make decisions as to the extent of cover to be given to the members based upon the underwriting and financial policy of the club. So far as the day-to-day operation and running of the club is concerned the members appoint professional managers who, under the guidance and instruction of the directors, deal with such matters as underwriting, rating of members, handling of claims and, most important, ensuring that the members receive all necessary assistance.

The most important aspect of the clubs' function is their service to their members. The clubs provide assistance to their members which goes very far beyond the payment of claims. The managers and their correspondents, whom they appoint throughout the world, and who include both commercial correspondents and lawyers, give in-depth assistance, and in many cases take over completely the handling of claims.

They also give advice on various aspects of documentation, technical advice, such as problems that may be met by shipowners with the carriage of certain commodities, and they are ready to take any action necessary to help members on a world-wide basis. Thus for a vessel requiring assistance, whether it be a cargo problem or sickness of a crew member, the shipowner may find such assistance in virtually any port of the world.

With regard to the question of claims handling, great importance is attached to the centralised control of claims, which enables the association to take note of changing patterns of such claims, thus ensuring that the members' interests are fully protected by taking appropriate measures as early as possible.

Once notice of a claim has been given by the member, the club will assume control of such claim by appointing surveyors, lawyers, or other professional advisers, as necessary. Depending on the merits of such claims action will be taken for settlement or possibly be defended in arbitration or Court proceedings; however, it must be noted that there is close consultation between the member and the club throughout.

With any situation that develops there is one particularly important service afforded by the clubs and that is the arranging of guarantees or letters of undertaking in order that an entered ship may be released from arrest or from the threat of arrest. However, it should be noted that a member does not have an automatic right to such guarantees as there is nothing in the rules providing for them, but they are very often provided and in this way security can usually be arranged extremely quickly, this being sufficient to release the ship.

The club covers the shipowners' liabilities to third parties, meaning, in this context, anybody other than the insured shipowner himself. The club does *not* cover—

loss of or damage to the entered ship,
loss of freight or hire,
demurrage or detention,
war risks.

Crew members, etc.

Cover is given for loss of life, personal injury claims, hospital, medical and funeral expenses. Repatriation expenses and the costs of sending substitutes to a ship are also covered in certain circumstances. If seamen lose personal effects as a result of a marine peril the club will reimburse the owners for the payments they have to make.

Death or injury of a person on an entered vessel because of the negligent management or navigation of the ship may result in a claim for damages from the shipowner. Stevedores slipping on a greasy deck, a passenger tripping on a loose stairway or a Customs official falling from a defective gangway; all are examples of accidents covered by the club.

Cargo

Many types of cargo are carried in a great many varieties of ship. Under the international convention known as the Hague Rules, now Hague-Visby Rules, and the statutes in other countries, shipowners have a duty carefully to load, stow, carry and deliver the cargo and if they fail to do so they may be liable in damages to the owners of the cargo. There is often contamination between different products carried on tankers, perhaps a crew member will have left open a valve or there may be a residue of cargo in the ship's lines. All such occurrences will be covered by the club. Sometimes in a case of General Average (e.g. a stranding or a fire) where there has been special sacrifice or expenditure in order that the voyage may be completed, the cargo interests might refuse to pay their proportion of General Average. They may say in such circumstances that the vessel was responsible for the occurrence and may seek to avoid paying their proportion to the General Average by alleging that the vessel was unseaworthy. In this situation the shipowner could recover from the club such contribution.

Fines

Ships can be subject to fines for a number of reasons; pollution by oil, smoke or garbage, breaches of immigration regulations, errors in the ship's manifest, even for crew members smuggling drugs, tobacco or alcohol. The amounts can be very large and the attitude of the authorities arbitrary. The owners will usually have no involvement but there is nevertheless a liability because of the neglect or deliberate act of his servants.

Contractual liabilities

Some people would say that contractual liabilities are not true third party liabilities, but cargo claims as previously mentioned often arise out of a breach of the contract of carriage. Furthermore, the club has for many years covered the liabilities arising under towage contracts. In many countries of the world a shipowner can engage tugs only on the basis that the shipowner in most circumstances is responsible for any damage done during the course of such towage operation. In recent years owners of facilities provided to ships, e.g. terminal areas, dry docks, floating cranes, have sought to put an increasing burden of responsibility on the shoulders of shipowners, even for accidents which are caused by the negligence of the owners of the facility. If the owners wish to, or have to, enter into such contracts they can have cover from the club provided the managers have given their approval to such contract.

Wreck removal

Often after a serious casualty, such as collision, stranding, fire or capsizing, local authorities or governments will demand that the shipowner remove the wreck of the ship, particularly if it is a hazard to navigation. Such cases can be difficult and costly, sometimes involving cutting up the ship piece by piece. In some countries by statute law there is no monetary limit which protects the shipowner from the cost of such an operation.

The most important advice that can be given to any party faced with a problem, whether he be the shipowner or his agent, is to seek advice from the club on any matter which may be giving concern in order that the correct decisions be taken speedily.

CHAPTER 8

DRY CARGO CHARTER-PARTIES

Main types

1. *TIME charter-party*

This constitutes an agreement whereunder a shipowner hires or "lets out" his ship to the charterer who has the liberty under the charter-party to use and employ the vessel for a stipulated period of time subject possibly to agreed trading limits or to restrictions on the types of goods to be carried. In consideration of the use of the vessel the charterer pays hire to the owner usually monthly in advance though arrangements can vary. Forms most commonly in use are (a) BALTIME 1939 and (b) New York Produce Exchange.

2. *VOYAGE charter-party*

This is an agreement whereunder the charterer engages a vessel to carry a specified cargo or cargoes on a specified voyage between two or more ports. He may or may not be the owner of the goods. In consideration of thus using the vessel he pays freight money to the owner either at an agreed rate per ton of cargo carried or on a fixed "lumpsum" basis. There are many special charter-party forms applying to the carriage of specialist cargoes but the commonly used form covering the carriage of general cargo is codenamed GENCON.

3. *DEMISE charter-party*

This is an agreement under the terms of which the ownership of the vessel to all intents and purposes, though not absolutely, passes to the charterer during the currency of the charter. Such an agreement is sometimes known as a BAREBOAT charter. One difference between a time charter and a demise charter is that the former gives no property interest to the charterer. The latter, however, is tantamount to, though just short of, an outright transfer of ownership. Anything less than that is either a time or voyage charter or not a charter-party at all.

One of the significant features of the demise charter is that the master and crew of the vessel are engaged, employed and paid by the charterer which involves the attributing of vicarious (employer's) liability for their acts, neglects and defaults to the demise charterer and not the actual owner. The owner thus remains very much in the background, merely receiving his monthly entitlement of charter hire. An apt comparison would be the relationship between the freehold owner of land and the leasehold/occupier of that same land. To identify a charter-party agreement as a demise charter it is essential that the wording of it must express a clear intent by the ship's owner that he has given over not only his permission to employ the ship but also has given over the management of the ship for the currency of the charter.

Another essential distinguishing feature between demise and time charters is that under a time charter the owner remains legally in possession of his ship through the medium of the master and crew (his servants) whereas under a demise form of charter he does not.

It is worth noting that charter agreements are often fixed on what, on first sight, look like "hybrid" charter-party terms, that is a "confusion" of the two types (time and voyage). Thus a "trip" charter which, for example, could be an agreement whereunder a ship performs a round trip carrying specified cargoes for a period of approximately six months.

Time charter-party (Specimen for discussion—"BALTIME 1939")

The agreement contains 25 clauses set out after the preamble containing the vessel's description and the identities of owner and charterer.

Clause 1 lays down the agreed hire period, the port or place where the ship is to be delivered to the charterer and the time of delivery.

Clause 2 sets out any limitation on trading areas which the owner may wish to impose on the charterer, e.g. for political reasons an owner might wish to exclude Cuba or for physical reasons the Arctic regions.

Clauses 3 and 4 lay down what it is expected owners will provide and charterers will provide respectively. Clause 4 is naturally larger than Clause 3 and lists in considerable detail all the individual voyage expenses likely to be incurred during the charter period.

Clause 5 deals with bunkers—quantity at delivery and redelivery and the payment therefor.

Clause 6 stipulates the agreed monetary payment by way of hire. It is customary for charterers to pay this hire by monthly or half-monthly instalments in advance. The clause includes penalty wording which confers on owners the right to withdraw their vessel if the charterers default in payment. The current law on this point as defined by the House of Lords is that the right accrues at the moment of default and the charterer by late payment cannot remove the accrued right. However, the owners must conversely give reasonably prompt notice and take action to withdraw, failing which they may be deemed to have waived their right to do so. (*The Laconia* [1977] 1 All E.R. 545.)

In recent times what have become known as "anti-technicality" clauses have been added in so as to temper the strictness of the established law and to avoid the right of withdrawal being too akin to a sort of sudden forfeiture. Such clauses allow for a period of say 48 hours to be granted by the owners to the charterer to "pay up" before withdrawal is finally exercised.

Clause 7 stipulates terms for redelivery and time and place. It also goes on to provide that charterers are obliged to give notice of redelivery. Much litigation has taken place on the question of marginal dates and flexibility in redelivery dates, with particular emphasis on the practice of charterers sending vessels on what has become known as an "illegal last voyage". The parties can stipulate for exact redelivery dates or not but if they do not the law will imply a reasonable margin if a reasonable margin is itself not specifically agreed. As to when the owner has the right to insist on payment of the current market rate if higher than the charter rate for late delivery, this depends on what is considered a reasonably or unreasonably delayed delivery date.

Clause 8 formally places the cargo spaces at the charterer's disposal.

Clause 9 defines the master's position. It should be remembered that under time charter-party terms the master remains the owners' legal servant but is placed under the direction and orders of the charterer so far as the employment of the ship is concerned. This clause is sometimes known as the "employment and indemnity clause" and it is the indemnity aspect of it which places great exposure on a charterer who orders the master to sign contractual documents which result in adverse consequences to owners. The expression "all liabilities" has been interpreted strictly in favour of owners, the Courts having defined the phrase as imposing an obligation to indemnify against the incurring of the *liability* rather than the indemnifying of payment made in discharge of a liability (*Bosma* v. *Larsen* [1966] 1 Lloyd's Rep. 22). The right to indemnity under this clause is, however, contingent on the establishment of a direct causal connection between the ultimate loss and the master's obeying of the charterer's orders (*The White Rose* [1969] 2 Lloyd's Rep. 52). The clause is strictly limited to matters of employment and does not entitle the charterer to any say in the navigation of the ship. That remains exclusively in the hands of the master and his owners.

The second paragraph of the clause provides the charterer with some measure of control over the master's conduct in that the charterer is provided at least with the right to voice dissatisfaction and require the owners to look into the matter. The actual making of a change in the appointment of a ship's officer in pursuance of this entitlement is rare.

Clause 10 is brief, to the point, unambiguous and self-explanatory.

Clause 11, colloquially known as the "off-hire" clause, defines, with very little cause for doubt, the circumstances in which the charterer is relieved from the obligation to pay hire during the charter period. The following points are specially emphasised: (a) "Deficiency of men" means deficiency in numbers. It does not mean, nor is construed to mean, inefficiency or incompetence of the crew who are provided. (*Greek Government* v. *Ministry of Transport* [1949] 1 All E.R. 171.) (b) The prevention of the working of the vessel must be determined in the light of how and why the charterer wishes to use the vessel at that point of time when the disablement occurs. Thus, if the ship's engines are disabled at a time when the vessel is working cargo alongside a wharf, the charterer is not thereby deprived of the use of the vessel at that particular time. Conversely, if a ship's winch is inoperative in the course of her voyaging at sea, that is not such a breakdown as will prevent or hinder the working of the vessel at that moment. It has been concisely said that it is the obligation of the owner to provide the ship and crew to work her and to provide the service then required by the charterer. (*The Apollo* [1978] 1 Lloyd's Rep. 200.) (c) If the vessel breaks down but is restored to efficiency within 24 hours no hire may be withheld. But if the disablement continues for more than 24 hours the off-hire period commences from the initial moment of disablement, not from 24 hours after the initial moment. (d) Any ambiguity shall be construed against the party seeking the benefit of the clause. (e) The scope and intent of the idea of "disablement" was clarified in the *H.R. Macmillan* case ([1974] 1 Lloyd's Rep. 311) which concerned the breakdown of Munck gantry cranes on the vessel. It did not cover the voluntary taking out of service of cranes for inspection and repair.

Clause 12 deals with regular boiler cleaning which is essential to the good maintenance of the vessel. Such activity is obviously in the joint interests of owner and charterer alike and the stipulation is put in clear terms and rightly is the subject of a separate clause.

Clause 13 is possibly one of the most invoked and disputed stipulations in the entire document. Perhaps the point which requires the most emphasis is that it is only the acts, faults or omissions of the owners or their *manager* which imposes liability on the owners, *not* of their servants or agents. The wording of the clause on the face of it would seem to read rather more in favour of owners than charterers, particularly with the additional second paragraph.

It is considered that the combination of clauses 9 and 13 is designed to cope comprehensively with the contractual "triangular" situation/relationship (i.e. shipowner, charterer and third party bill of lading holder) from the angle both of the owner and of the charterer, whichever is found ultimately liable to the third party.

Clause 14 is self-explanatory.

Clause 15 contains a provision on an "ad hoc" basis additional to any general trading limits which may be imposed by clause 2 and which further controls the charterer's liberties to order the vessel where he pleases.

Clause 16 is self-explanatory. The wording clearly copes with the extreme likelihood of the exact date of loss being impossible of determination.

Clause 17. The often excessive overtime pay scales make it natural that charterers should be fully responsible by express agreement for such expenses if overtime work is ordered for their exclusive benefit.

Clause 18 is a mutually protective clause, but the very nature of this type of lien— i.e. dependent entirely upon possession—makes effective exercise of the lien frequently difficult. Withholding delivery of cargoes in exercise of a lien, particularly where government interests are the rightful consignees, has often been found impossible and this reduces the strength of the lien to be "paper value" only. However, the inclusion of a lien clause is generally of great importance to an owner, particularly if the charterer's reputation and financial standing is questionable.

Clause 19. Salvage rewards are, under the general maritime law of salvage, customarily for the vessel's legal owners, her master and crew, but as this clause illustrates a time charterer may by express agreement share in the benefits. Since any salvage agreement is normally signed by the master, his signature would not only bind the owners but also taking into account the last sentence of this clause impose defined obligations on the charterer as well. Equal sharing of out-of-pocket expenses and salvage reward is agreed. This entire clause is quite consistent with the very equitable nature of the law of salvage generally.

Clause 20. Subletting is a very common practice and it is not uncommon to have a lengthy "chain" of charter-parties possibly even including "back to back" charters. The basic rule remains, however, that the original charterer remains fully responsible to the owner. This coincides with the basic doctrine of privity of contract by which no third party can be bound legally under the terms and conditions of a contract between first and second parties.

Clause 21. The importance and protective benefit of this stipulation is the more enhanced by the ever increasing likelihood of "short-notice" localised wars or hostilities and the examples since the Second World War are numerous—Korea, Suez 1956, Vietnam, India/Pakistan, Arab/Israeli. It is of vital importance that no ship's master should be placed in a seemingly insoluble dilemma bearing in mind his "two-hatted" position when under time charter of being the owners' servant/employee and yet under the orders and direction of the charterers as regards employment of ship. That an innocent ship and/or her cargo should, through no fault of her owner or even perhaps charterer, find herself caught up in a war zone is unconscionable and any contract which did not make adequate provision for such a foreseeable situation would be singularly lacking.

The "safety valve" sub-section applicable to a situation where one party to the agreement is a person whose country has become directly involved in liability is an offshoot perhaps of the general contractual rule of frustration. In other words, such an event might be construed simply as a supervening event destroying the original purpose and intention of the parties.

As to what is a "government" within the wording of the War Risks Clause, the English Courts gave their view in a case referred to them by an umpire in 1956 involving the Italian steamship *Maribu*. This unfortunate vessel had found herself intercepted by a Formosan Government warship whilst innocently proceeding on a cargo voyage from North China to Europe. She was taken to Keelung where her cargo was discharged. She was released and the charter voyage abandoned. The ship's owners claimed balance of freight. In answering the question as to whether the ship had complied with the orders of "any other government" the English Court said that it is not the exclusive view of the British Government that is the criterion for determination but rather the test is "was the national government of the country concerned in exercise of full executive and legislative control and power over an established territory". The Formosan Government was such a government in those terms, they said. (*Luigi Monta* v. *Cechofracht Co. Ltd.* [1956] 2 Lloyd's Rep. 97.)

N.B. It is important to distinguish between what is an "act of war" and what is merely the consequence or aftermath arising from war. The Hague or Hague-Visby Rules talk of the exception of "Act of war" and in the next breath of "Act of public enemies". One can only interpret from these two separate exceptions that to be a war there must be an official declaration of hostilities and that anything else or anything short of that would be an act of public enemies—viz. a terrorist bomb in London docks causing damage to goods under a bill of lading would be an act of public enemies.

Clause 22. See **Voyage** charter-parties for comments on this type of clause. There is no *contractual* right available to the charterer to cancel until the cancelling date has been reached. This is so even if it is clear that the shipowner will not be able to deliver the ship in time. But the charterer does have a common law remedy of rescission alleging that the contract has been frustrated or there has been an anticipatory breach of contract.

Clause 23. Arbitration is an immense subject, difficult to condense. Businessmen have generally always seemed to prefer their disputes to be resolved by men of their own standing—commercial men—who are inclined to apply a more practical mind and commercial considerations to the issues. The standard arbitration clause in the Baltime form is the simplest wording which can be found. There is no limitation period fixed so that each party is allowed six years from the arising of the cause of action in which to appoint his arbitrator. This is the common law and indeed the statutory limitation period applicable to all contracts. London is the most popular of the world's centres of arbitration, closely followed by New York. Other centres are Paris, Peking, Athens, Montreal, Oslo. Arbitrators, who are basically finders of fact, cannot be challenged regarding an alleged error of fact, but only regarding an alleged error of law in the award. This is one of the more significant innovations introduced by the 1979 Arbitration Act which was intended to place restriction on the extent of judicial review of arbitration awards. The "special case stated" procedure, allowed under the 1950 Act, has been abolished and a straightforward system of appeal to the High Court substituted.

Clause 24. General Average arrangements. This one-line clause is entirely self-explanatory. The York/Antwerp rules were revised in 1974 when some eight of the rules were modified.

Clause 25. Brokers, though not principal parties, have nevertheless very rightly protection re their commission under this clause.

The Voyage charter-party (The Gencon)

Clause 1 sets out details of the vessel, the identity of the parties, the place of loading, the type of cargo, the destination and the freight money payable for the carriage. A charter-party which stipulates that the vessel carries its cargo to a named dock or berth will be known as a "dock" or "berth" charter. Where a port or ports only is/are stipulated as destination(s) then the document is known as a "port" charter. (For the legal effects of the difference see later under "Laytime".) Freight may by agreement be paid on a per ton basis or alternatively as a lumpsum. Lumpsum freight is payable in full regardless of how much cargo is finally delivered at destination provided that some of it is delivered. Under the common law rule freight is payable only on "right and true" delivery. "Right and true" does not imply necessarily in *perfect* condition but rather in conformity with the agreements re time and place. In practice the method and time of paying freight is varied by express agreement, e.g. 20% after completion of loading, 50% on "breaking bulk" and balance on final delivery.

A charterer generally warrants that a destination port is "safe". A port is "safe" if an ordinarily prudent and skilful master can find a way of reaching it in safety. Thus it can be seen conversely that a port is *not* safe if, although safe in itself, it cannot be reached in safety. The whole question should be viewed in the light of the particular ship involved and in respect of it being properly manned, equipped, navigated and handled with good seamanship (see *The Polyglory* [1977] 2 Lloyd's Rep. 353).

Lord Denning has recently suggested that a test in these modern times should be whether or not the "set-up" in the port concerned is safe as a working system, i.e. the ancillary services available and ready. A case in point was disputed a short while ago in which a shipowner failed to recover from the charterer the costs of hiring two port tugs to keep his ship on the berth allocated to him. Adverse currents were influencing the vessel away from the berth designated by the charterer. Such damages were not properly recoverable under the safe berth warranty principles.

Clause 2 defines the scope of the owner's responsibilities and bears a marked similarity to clause 13 of the Baltime charter-party, the equivalent clause. In the same way as far as concerns the responsibility for the consequences of unseaworthiness it restricts the owner's responsibility to his own or his manager's lack of due diligence. The owner's liability is excluded in the event the unseaworthiness is wholly due to the fault or omission of his servants or agents.

Clause 3. The popular "liberty" clause. If the Hague Rules or subsequent variations of the Rules are expressly incorporated into the charter-party this clause will be construed in accordance with what will be deemed a reasonable deviation under the circumstances.

Clause 4. The wording reflects the common law rule that freight is paid on delivery. The advance of cash for disbursements should not be confused with an advance of freight. Regardless of whatever may be the charter-party wording the test is usually who has the responsibility of effecting insurance on the freight. By applying this test it can be determined who had the interest at the time, for instance, the ship and cargo is totally lost before full performance of the contract and thus whether an advance of money was merely a loan or was an actual part payment of freight.

Clauses 5 and 6 give details of laytime allowed to the charterer for loading and/or discharging the cargo. Laytime is the time allowed to the charterer to use the ship to load or discharge the charter cargo free of extra charge beyond the payment of the stipulated freight.

Notice of readiness, usually in letter form though this is not legally required, is given by the master officially tendering his vessel as ready to load or discharge. Before laytime can start the vessel must be an "arrived" ship. Under a "berth" or "dock" charter this means she must have reached the berth or dock named in the charter-party. Under a "port" charter-party the determining of whether or not the ship is arrived so as to validate the notice of readiness and thus the commencement of running of laytime is subject to a test. The current test was laid down by the House of Lords in 1973 (*The Johanna Oldendorff* [1973] 2 Lloyd's Rep. 285) and is in two parts:—

    a. the vessel must have reached a customary waiting area within the port and

    b. must be at the immediate and effective disposal of the charterer. (See also *The Maratha Envoy* case [1977] 2 Lloyd's Rep. 301.)

It is customary by contract for there to be an interval elapsing between the tendering of the notice of readiness and the commencement of laytime. This is sometimes called "notice" time and may be used by the charterer. As to who bears the expense may be expressly agreed in this same clause.

Each clause concludes with the words "time lost in waiting for a berth to count as loading/discharging time". The effect of these words is to counterbalance the effect of the "arrived ship" rule which tends to construe a charter-party in favour of the charterer if the words do not appear. Where in a charter-party the time lost provisions are independent of the laytime provisions the latter do not affect the former (*The Radnor* [1955] 2 Lloyd's Rep. 668). In the *Loucas N.* ([1970] 2 Lloyd's Rep. 482) it was said that the time lost provisions applied *before* the vessel arrived and the laytime provisions applied *after* the ship had become an "arrived" ship. Thus the two seemingly contrasting sets of provisions could be reconciled within the same charter-party agreement.

In 1976 (*The Darrah* case [1976] 1 Lloyd's Rep. 285) the House of Lords gave relief to charterers by holding that laytime exceptions should be applied even to the waiting time.

As the law presently stands (a) there is no conflict between the laytime provisions and the time lost provisions in the case of an *arrived* ship under a *port* charter-party and (b) the shipowner does not gain a greater advantage from his ship being kept waiting for a berth than he would get from her being kept at her berth.

Clause 7. Demurrage is a fixed penalty (liquidated damages) the amount being agreed and stipulated in the charter-party, paid by the charterer to the owner for delaying the ship beyond the expiry of the agreed laytime. It is not, therefore, *technically* damages for breach of contract. It is usually for a fixed period though not necessarily. Laytime exceptions do not apply to the demurrage period so that the principle of "once on demurrage always on demurrage" is of universal application to the charterer's detriment unless the wording is sufficiently clear (very rare) to allow him the benefit of laytime excepted periods even after laytime has expired. Though not specifically mentioned it is customary for owners to pay "despatch money" to charterers (usually at half the demurrage rate) as reward for finishing the vessel in advance of the termination of laytime.

Three conditions must be satisfied before laytime can commence under the ordinary terms and conditions of any voyage charter-party on whatever form:

    a. the vessel must be an "arrived" ship.

    b. she must have presented a notice of readiness.

    c. the vessel must *in all respects* be ready to load (or discharge as the case may be).

Owner and charterer are at liberty to come to any private arrangement they wish about who has the benefit of the time between the tendering of the notice of readiness and the commencement of laytime, if indeed it is used. One customary arrangement is that it counts as "half time", if used.

Clause 8. Lien. Under the common law and independent of any contractual arrangement a shipowner has the right to retain possession of goods (a possessory lien) as security for the payment of freight (but only if the freight is entirely payable at the common law time—that is, on "right and true delivery"), General Average contributions and salvage contributions. A shipowner has no lien, however, at common law for any other charges. Thus if a vessel owner wants to protect his interests in respect of possible unpaid demurrage, damages for detention, deadfreight or other charges, he must insert an express lien clause in the charter-party.

This protection by the shipowner becomes of increased importance if the charterer seeks, as he frequently does, to protect his own interests by inserting a "cesser" clause in the charter-party allowing him to opt out of any further responsibilities once the cargo has physically been loaded. A charterer who has no property interest in the goods is likely to have such a clause inserted. The Courts have generally considered that the lien clause (for owners' protection) should be co-extensive with the cesser clause (charterers' protection).

N.B. Damages for detention differs from demurrage in that the former is a claim against the charterer assessed on its merits and arising as a result of a charterer's breach of contract in delaying a vessel unreasonably. It is usually applicable if there are no demurrage stipulations at all (most unusual) or if even the stipulated demurrage period has been exceeded and the vessel is still detained. Damages for detention is described as *un*liquidated damages and is based on two things, the daily running cost of the vessel and any foreseeable loss of profit suffered by the shipowner as a direct consequence of the detention.

Clause 9. Another protective clause in favour of the shipowner bearing in mind that the ship's master is the shipowner's legal servant and that the original bills of lading will almost certainly be negotiated to a third party receiver for value.

Clause 10. The Cancelling Clause. One significant point here is that there can be no anticipatory breach of contract in respect of this clause. Until the cancelling date has been reached there is no *contractual* right vested in the charterer to cancel. Even if it is quite clear that the ship cannot make the nominated port by the cancelling date the ship is still under an obligation to proceed. Any right which either party may have is granted by common law only. If under such circumstances the charterer does cancel and the shipowner unqualifiedly accepts the cancellation then this is considered to be a separate arrangement mutually agreed. Conversely, after the cancelling date is reached, the shipowner has no right to require the charterer to declare whether or not he wishes to load. The charterer must not, however, allow an unreasonable time to elapse before declaring his option.

N.B. Exceptions clauses in the charter-party operating in the shipowner's favour refer to the *carrying* voyage and do not apply in his favour to the *approach* voyage to loading port.

Clause 11. It should be noted that the York/Antwerp Rules were revised in 1974. In connection with the last sentence of this clause the provisions of the New Jason clause (explained elsewhere) if incorporated into the contract should be borne in mind.

Clause 12. Many people are mystified as to why this clause still survives in the printed charter-party form. It is anachronistic, unrealistic, is regarded as inoperative and the Courts quite rightly disregard it. It is a relic which survives only perhaps because of the English love of tradition and conservatism and for no other practical reason. Non-performance means just what it says and does not include within its meaning poor, inefficient, bad or faulty performance. Student and practitioner alike can, therefore, safely ignore it.

Clauses 13 and 14. These are self-explanatory.

The Ice Clause. The effect of the incidence of ice-bound weather conditions on a carriage contract depends quite naturally on whether the condition constitutes a permanent or only a temporary obstruction to the performance of the contract and this can only be decided in each case on its merits bearing in mind that a charter-party is above all a commercial document in the sense that it sets out the aims and intentions of commercial persons in a business deal. Thus what constitutes inordinate delay as a result of ice-bound conditions is relative in each case to the nature of the individual contract.

A port may be inaccessible due to ice at the time when the ship approaches to load but if in the normal course of events the ice would clear in, say, three days, *not* to wait would be construed as *un*reasonable under the circumstances. The ice clause, therefore, provides liberties to the master who may be in genuine fear of being frozen in for an unduly long time to sail with or without cargo with impunity. Yet another clause to set a master's mind at rest!

At the discharge port end the clause gives the receiver the option to keep the ship waiting if there is ice obstruction and paying due demurrage or of ordering the ship to an alternative convenient and accessible port. Such alternative is no breach of contract and all the terms and conditions of the contract will continue to apply. There is, however, one interesting little proviso that if the distance between the named port of discharge and the substituted port exceeds 100 nautical miles the freight charges may be increased in proportion.

Neither ice clause (loading or discharge) has any application in the spring.

The General Strike Clause. A strike is one of many causes of an interruption of work causing delay and thus financial loss to one or other party. A strike can be defined as a concerted refusal by workmen to work in support of an alleged grievance against their employers—usually for more money or better conditions. Rarely does a strike occur through the fault of either contracting party. Excluded from the foregoing definition of a strike would be a situation where crew, in order to induce a shipowner to satisfy claims lodged by them, might refuse to allow longshoremen to discharge a ship. Nor will the stoppage of work by men merely because of fear of disease be a strike within the meaning of the strike clause.

The strike must directly or proximately cause the delay and if a charterer fails to take the opportunity to avoid the consequences of a strike he will lose the protection of the strike clause exceptions. If the strike was too remote and so far removed in the "chain of causation" from the actual consequences resulting in delay, the benefits of the clause cannot be reaped.

A charterer who could have prevented a strike and/or its consequences cannot thereafter invoke a strike exception clause in his favour. Also he must take any reasonable measures to mitigate his losses as a result of delay, particularly in the aftermath of a strike.

One of the most celebrated "strike" cases litigated in recent years—*Reardon Smith Line* v. *Ministry of Agriculture* [1963] 1 Lloyd's Rep. 12—allowed the charterers the benefit of strike clause exceptions in a situation where a strike of grain elevator men at Vancouver had prevented wheat being loaded from elevators in the port generally when large numbers of vessels were waiting to load that commodity. The drastic nature of the situation caused the authorities to order the loading of the liner vessels as priority and the tramps were kept waiting. Thus the consequence of emergency measures taken by reason of a strike were tantamount to the effect of the strike itself for the purposes of the interpretation of the particular strike provisions in that charter-party contract.

CHAPTER 9

PASSENGER CONTRACTS

The nature of the contract

A contract of passage by sea is essentially one between an expert (the carrier) and a non-expert (the passenger). The printed terms and conditions on a passage ticket, usually in minute print, have long included exceptions from and limitation of liability heavily weighted in the carrier's favour. Commonly found in such tickets has been the exclusion from liability clause in respect of death or injury howsoever caused whether or not by the negligence of the carrier's servants or agents.

Original legal thinking on the passage contract

The rationale of acceptance of the contract terms by the sea passenger was originally based on (and this was confirmed by the Courts in certain railway and hotel cases in which the facts and circumstances were very similar to sea passage cases) the physical handing over of the ticket to the passenger in exchange for the passage money. Whether he understood or even knew of the existence of the terms printed on his ticket seemed in the very early days to be irrelevant—he was contractually bound by them. This apparently harsh doctrine may well have been founded on the basis of the long-cherished British tradition and respect for freedom of contract between individuals. The ticket itself was, thus, the contractual document.

How the law developed

In 1955 an opportunity arose to temper in a sense the previous harshness of the legal rules. The significant case of *Adler* v. *Dickson* ([1955] 1 Q.B. 158) was decided. The facts were that a widow enjoying a cruise on the passenger ship *Himalaya* suffered injury. Her passage ticket contained a complete exclusion from liability clause so, taking legal advice, she sued the ship's master and/or bo'sun (boatswain) alleging negligence and won her case. This ruling showed that whereas the carrier could thoroughly protect himself by express exclusion clauses the protection did not extend to his servants/agents who were exposed to action direct from the third party passenger.

This case gave birth to the now widely known and used "Himalaya Clause" used in bills of lading and which purports to allow the benefits of the contract terms to be conferred also on the servants or agents of the carrier (of goods).

Continuing development

The harshness of the law, so unfavourable to the "innocent" passenger, became gradually tempered judicially by the revised thinking that the delivery of the ticket was not necessarily the moment when the contract was concluded so as to bind both parties. The rule that the terms and conditions of the contract, or at least the more significant of them, should be drawn to the attention of the prospective passenger at the time when he enters into negotiations to book his passage became an obligation of the prospective carrier through his agent. Failure to do this would lose him the benefit of his protective clauses. This reasoning took time, however, to achieve the Courts' unqualified recognition. The 1960s and 1970s nevertheless did see the Courts' reaction swing quite far in the passenger's favour.

The Hollingworth case ([1977] 2 Lloyd's Rep. 70)

Failure to bring the terms and conditions of the passage contract sufficiently to the passenger's notice at the time of booking the passage so as to give the passenger the opportunity not to go ahead with the booking if he was dissatisfied defeated the carrier's attempts to rely on the contractual terms if a cause of action, for example, for damages for death or injury, subsequently arose against him. The *Hollingworth* dispute was litigated more on the basis of whether the carrier was at fault through failure to take due care or alternatively in breach of a statutory duty as the occupier of premises upon which people entered as business "invitees".

The Occupier's Liability Act 1957

This statute made it obligatory for shipowners to take reasonable care that their ship(s) and its (their) equipment were safe for the carriage of passengers.

No common law warranty of seaworthiness

Under the common law of England there is no evidence that there is any warranty of seaworthiness of the carrying vessel owed by the carrier of passengers to the passenger and implied into the passage contract. In this respect the common law differs from the common law applying to contracts to carry goods by sea.

Recent developments

(a) The Unfair Contract Terms Act 1977

This Act was brought into effect in February, 1978. Parts of it apply to England and Wales and another part to Scotland. It is now not possible for a shipowner/carrier of passengers validly to exclude his liability for death or injury during carriage. Under section 2 of the Act it is not permitted to exclude liability for negligence, the consequences of which directly results in death or personal injury. The statute applies to many types of contract and the main intent of the Act is to make all seemingly unfair clauses subject to a test of "reasonableness" according to the status of the two contracting parties and bearing in mind their relative "bargaining power" at the time when they entered into the contract. Particularly affected are contracts for the sale of goods. Passenger contracts are affected to the extent described above and this is yet another development in the trend of the law towards balancing more evenly the respective rights and liabilities of carrier and passenger. The Act also makes reference in its text to the Athens Convention.

(b) The Athens Convention

This is a 1974 Convention on carriage of passengers and their baggage by sea. Countries have been slow to adopt it although Britain has ratified it by incorporating it as Schedule 3 to the Merchant Shipping Act 1979. This part of the Act was brought into effect on Jan. 1, 1981.

Main intent and provisions of the Convention

One of its principal aims is the tight control of exception clauses. The basis of liability should be simply *fault*, the burden of so proving being on the passenger. The burden should only be reversed in the event of injury or death or loss of baggage resulting from shipwreck, collision, stranding, explosion, fire or defect in the vessel (Article 3).

The Convention also defines limits of liability available to the carrier of passengers and their baggage (Articles 7 and 8). The figures laid down are Poincaré francs as in the other recent international maritime Conventions and 700,000 francs is the amount to which limitation may be fixed for death or injury. Other limits listed in the Articles are 12,500 Poincaré francs for cabin baggage (if not in or on a vehicle), 50,000 for a vehicle plus baggage in or on it, and 18,000 for other luggage. A significant feature is that the right to limit will only be denied to the carrier if he is proved guilty of reckless conduct or deliberate misconduct from which he knew loss or damage or harm would result if he acted so (Article 13, section 1). Servants or agents of the carrier who may generally avail themselves of the benefits, defences, etc., available to the carrier will also be prevented from limiting their liability if sued direct in the event of similar conduct by them.

Legal action for damages may be brought within two years of disembarkation. Failure to do so will render the action "time barred". If it is a death, then the time will run from the moment when the deceased passenger should have disembarked.

CHAPTER 10

LIMITATION OF LIABILITY

Original idea

To saddle owners of ships with unlimited liability for loss or damage to other persons or their property was thought to be likely to discourage the business of seafaring generally and to endanger thereby the flourishing of international trade. A serious maritime disaster in olden times could easily bankrupt the owner of the offending vessel. Possibly his only alternative would have been to abandon his ship and cargo into the hands of his creditors—a practical form, some would say, of limiting liability anyway.

In the maritime world disasters can usually be contained within the industry itself, which cannot necessarily be said of the air industry. This is a supporting argument to the theory of limitation in maritime claims. Another pro-limitation argument was that it is not unjust that a person should be responsible for *fully* compensating his victims suffering civil wrong through his own personal fault but there is less justice in a person being fully accountable when the fault is that of his servant or agent, i.e. his vicarious liability is involved. (Vicarious liability is the liability of an employer for the consequences of the acts, neglects or defaults of his employees.)

Although the ability to limit his liability in respect of maritime claims lodged against him whether based on contract or tort has been available for some four centuries, in Britain the form of limitation as we know it today was not established statutorily until 1894 when the original Merchant Shipping Act was passed. Part VIII is devoted to the subject and in particular section 503, which reads as follows:

> 503.—(1) The owners of a ship, British or foreign, shall not, where all or any of the following occurrences take place without their actual fault or privity; (that is to say,)
>
> (*a*) Where any loss of life or personal injury is caused to any person being carried in the ship;
>
> (*b*) Where any damage or loss is caused to any goods, merchandise, or other things whatsoever on board the ship;
>
> (*c*) Where any loss of life or personal injury is caused to any person carried in any other vessel by reason of the improper navigation of the ship;
>
> (*d*) Where any loss or damage is caused to any other vessel, or to any goods, merchandise, or other things whatsoever on board any other vessel, by reason of the improper navigation of the ship;
>
> be liable to damages beyond the following amounts; (that is to say,)
>
> (i) In respect of loss of life or personal injury, either alone or together with loss of or damage to vessels, goods, merchandise, or other things, an

aggregate amount not exceeding fifteen pounds for each ton of their ship's tonnage; and

(ii) In respect of loss of, or damage to, vessels, goods, merchandise, or other things, whether there be in addition loss of life or personal injury or not, an aggregate amount not exceeding eight pounds for each ton of their ship's tonnage.

(2) For the purposes of this section—

(a) The tonnage of a steam ship shall be her gross tonnage without deduction on account of engine room; and the tonnage of a sailing ship shall be her registered tonnage:

Provided that there shall not be included in such tonnage any space occupied by seamen or apprentices and appropriated to their use which is certified under the regulations scheduled to this Act with regard thereto.

(b) Where a foreign ship has been or can be measured according to British law, her tonnage, as ascertained by that measurement shall, for the purpose of this section, be deemed to be her tonnage.

(c) Where a foreign ship has not been and cannot be measured according to British law, the surveyor-general of ships in the United Kingdom, or the chief measuring officer of any British possession abroad, shall, on receiving from or by the direction of the court hearing the case, in which the tonnage of the ship is in question, such evidence concerning the dimensions of the ship as it may be practicable to furnish, give a certificate under his hand stating what would in his opinion have been the tonnage of the ship if she had been duly measured according to British law, and the tonnage so stated in that certificate shall, for the purposes of this section, be deemed to be the tonnage of the ship.

(3) The owner of every sea-going ship or share therein shall be liable in respect of every such loss of life, personal injury, loss of or damage to vessels, goods, merchandise, or things as aforesaid arising on distinct occasions to the same extent as if no other loss, injury, or damage had arisen.

Minor amendments were introduced in the intervening years until 1958 when a major amendment known as the Merchant Shipping (Liability of Shipowners and Others) Act was passed as a result of the Convention deposited the previous year, 1957, on Limitation of Liability of Seagoing Ships.

The system under which British shipowners operate differs from the only other commonly used system of limiting, that of the ruling market value of the ship, in that it is based on an amount calculated by multiplying a specified sum (originally pounds sterling now gold Poincaré francs) by the ship's tonnage figure. This establishes a fund which is eventually paid into Court and out of which all claims arising from the original accident are satisfied.

Loss of life and injury claims are given priority over claims in respect of damage to goods or property. If the aggregate of claims arising exceeds the amount of the fund, a *pro rata* distribution in settlement is made, taking into account the Merchant Shipping Act calculation. The current limitation calculation is based on the figure of 3,100 gold francs if loss of life, injury *and* property claims are involved and 1,000 gold francs if only property claims are involved.

A "Life" fund is formed by taking the first 2,100 gold francs and multiplying this by the ship's tonnage figure. Out of this will be satisfied the life and injury claims. If the aggregate exceeds the fund, then each claim is settled *pro rata* according to the same ratio as the aggregate bears to the fund.

> Example . . . (hypothetical):—
> Aggregate life/injury claims—1,000
> Life fund   700
> Claims settled on 7/10ths basis

The unsatisfied balance of 3/10ths of each claim comes down and ranks alongside (or "pari passu") with the property damage claims to be satisfied if possible out of the property fund which is formed by the multiplication of 1,000 gold francs by the ship's tonnage. Similarly, if this aggregate exceeds the fund, then these claims are settled *pro rata* only.

The right to limit liability is only available to a shipowner if he can show that the occurrence resulting in damage or harm took place without his own actual fault or privity. An application to the Court to limit must be made and the shipowner becomes the plaintiff and the defendant is any one of the claimants against him.

When ships became customarily owned by corporate entities rather than persons some difficulty arose in determining who in the corporate structure could be so closely identified with the owning company that his actions, neglects or defaults could be said to be that of the shipowner rather than of his servants or agents. Litigated cases on this point are numerous.

Tests Applied

(a) Whose was the controlling mind behind and/or who had the direction of the voyage in question?

(b) Would the mishap, calamity, damage not have occurred if that person had acted as a reasonable person under the circumstances?

An essential feature of the right to limit under section 503 of the Merchant Shipping Act 1894 as enlarged and amended by the 1958 Act is that the act or neglect causing the loss or damage must have been in the course of the navigation or management of the vessel. Thus the act of an employee engaged in underwater operations would fall outside the scope of section 503 and thus not entitle the ship's owner to limit (see

The Tojo Maru). *But* nevertheless the act need not have been performed *on board* the vessel provided that it was nevertheless in the course of navigation or management of the offending vessel.

The expression "carried on board the vessel" in respect of loss of life or personal injury claims is construed as meaning not necessarily physically on board at the time of the accident but the test is rather more was there some form of contractual relationship such as a passenger contract or a crew contract of employment on board. Thus a crewman injured when he is two steps down a ship's gangway could be construed as "carried on board" even though he was not at the time physically on board the ship itself.

An increase in those persons who could avail themselves of the statutory limitation benefits was made when the 1958 amendments were introduced. The original (1894) Act intended only the actual owner of the ship or its charterer by demise to have the benefits. Section 3(1) of the Merchant Shipping (Liability of Shipowners and Others) Act 1958 conferred entitlement also on:—

(a) A ship's master; (b) a member of the ship's crew; (c) a charterer whether by demise or purely on a time basis; (d) a ship's operator; (e) any person having an interest in or actually possessing a ship, i.e. a shipbuilder or perhaps a ship repairer.

A "ship", originally defined as any craft used in the course of navigation and not propelled by oars, was later extended also to include craft such as lighters or barges, however propelled, provided that they were used exclusively in non-tidal waters other than harbours. (Section 4(1) of the 1958 amendments deals with this point.)

Section 2(2) of the 1958 amendments introduces contingencies which are additional to the traditional primary ones. It provides for limitation to be available in respect of obligation or liability arising out of firstly the raising, removal or destruction of any ship which is sunk, stranded or abandoned or of anything on board such a ship, or, secondly, in respect of any damage (howsoever caused) to harbour works, basins or navigable waterways. Two significant points are:

(a) The sub-section is not yet in force and (b) the matter of wreck-raising expenses introduces the question as to whether they are truly damages within the meaning of the statutory limitation provisions or whether they are merely a statutory debt which comes into existence independently of any original fault, neglect or omission. The statutory debt concept is the doctrine usually embodied in local port authority statutes which empower a local authority which has raised a wreck to recover the costs of so doing from the wreck's owners. These arguments were fully discussed in *The Berwyn* ([1977] 2 Lloyd's Rep. 98) where it was decided that there were two causes of action, one for damages resulting from negligent navigation and the other to recover a statutory debt. Just as there were two causes of action, so a defending wreck owner must realise that he is obliged to limit on both *separately* and cannot merge his limitation on both into one.

The Limitation Fund

The gold franc became the basis upon which limitation fund sums were calculated because of its constancy and the ability to reassess sterling against it from time to time. The sterling equivalent is promulgated by the British Government at periodic intervals by Statutory Instruments. The stabilising of the Fund is guaranteed by the basic rule that after payment into Court of the Fund no subsequent alteration in the value of sterling as against the gold franc can affect the previously constituted Fund.

Interest rates

The old policy was to stick by the rigidity of fixed interest rates. Thus often out-of-date rates were used and unfairly prejudiced the parties' position. The tendency of the Courts these days is to reason that interest rates generally should be based on the notion that the party seeking limitation has prevented the various claimants from getting their money and retained the use of it himself. The rate of interest should be a matter for the Courts' discretion, there being no merit in the prolonged stabilisation of interest rates for whatever reason.

The position where tug and tow seek to limit

The rule here is based on where the negligent act arose which caused the loss or damage which has in turn given rise to the seeking of limitation. Also the statutory right to limit liability is available under agreed circumstances to a vessel owner (and others) only if *his own servants* have been at fault.

Thus where loss or damage is caused by a "tug and tow situation", if only those on board the tug are negligent and thereby the loss/damage is caused, the tug *only* limits in accordance with the tonnage of the tug. Conversely, where the tow and those on board her have been the cause of the damage through negligence, the tow's tonnage is the basis for the tow owner limiting. Where the negligence of those on board *both* craft is involved each owner limits in accordance with his own vessel's tonnage. This rule can easily be adapted and applied also where the tug and tow are in common ownership.

To conclude, mention should be made of the Convention on Limitation of Liability for Maritime Claims 1976 (the London Convention). It is likely that in the not too distant future the 1957 Limitation Convention will be replaced by the London Convention. That Britain fully intends to bring its provisions into effect is evidenced by the inclusion of the Convention's text into the Merchant Shipping Act 1979 as Schedule 4.

The main features of the London Convention are these:—

(a) A new concept for the denying of the right to limit will replace the "actual fault or privity" rule as contained in the 1957 Convention. The 1976 Convention contains the idea that a person attempting to limit his liability will be barred from doing so only if it is proved that it was a personal act or omission of his committed deliberately with the intent to cause such loss or so recklessly that the person who committed the act must be deemed to have knowledge that such loss would very likely result (Article 4).

(b) The actual figured limits of liability are based on units of account. The definition of a unit of account is laid down in Article 8 as being the special drawing right as defined and determined by the International Monetary Fund. Such units of account, in the same way as the Poincaré franc, are to be converted into the currency of whatever State has jurisdiction over the particular limitation proceedings.

(c) Salvors have at last under the 1976 Convention achieved recognition in their own right as opposed to merely being a "species" of shipowner. In Article 1 of the 1976 Convention, a salvor is described as any type of person rendering services in direct connection with salvage operations. This development in the law will be encouraging news for salvors who under the presently existing limitation laws find themselves exposed to the probability that they are unable to limit their liability due to the nature of their operations which might involve their employees' act, neglect or default which may have caused damage to maritime property being one not in the course of the navigation or management of the vessel (i.e. the salvage tug).

(d) Also provided for in Article 1 of the Convention is that an insurer of liability for claims subject to limitation in accordance with the rules of the Convention should be entitled to the benefits of the Convention to the same extent as the assured himself.

Generally speaking, the full text of the Convention may be found as scheduled to the Merchant Shipping Act 1979 and sections 17, 18 and 19 of the Act itself will eventually enable the Convention to be made effective in the United Kingdom. However, before there can be any bringing into effect of the Convention in the

United Kingdom so as to replace the 1957 Convention, it is required that the Convention itself must have been adopted by the minimum required number of sovereign States, that is 12.

Readers are reminded that claims in respect of oil pollution are dealt with under separate international Conventions. The right to limit in respect of claims in respect of passengers is dealt with also by a separate Convention (the Athens Convention of 1974).

CHAPTER 11

THE ROLE OF THE MASTER

The master of a ship must be a person capable of commanding respect and confidence from his employers as well as his subordinates and other personnel that he has to deal with during the course of a voyage. The shipowner relies on the master for the managing, in all its varied aspects, of his ship since the safety of the ship, cargo, passengers and crew are in his hands.

The role of the master may be divided into a number of separate categories as follows:—

(1) The Manager of a Commercial Enterprise;

(2) The Safety Officer; and,

(3) The Law Officer.

Frequently the master has to take all three roles at one and the same time since there are no clearly defined boundaries between them. In managing a ship as a commercial enterprise he must ensure the safety of the ship and cargo and at all times be able to command immediate obedience from the crew. Failure in any of these aspects may have serious consequences.

The above roles are outlined below under their separate headings:

(1) The Manager of a Commercial Enterprise

A ship, irrespective of its size, is a commercial undertaking or enterprise and although the shipowner has control over the movements of his ship, the cargoes loaded, etc., he is, however, dependent on the master to ensure the smooth and successful running of the shipboard side of the operation and the successful carrying out of his orders. Despite modern sophisticated methods of communication between ship and shore the ultimate responsibility for the efficient carrying out of this operation lies solely with the master. The master's various roles within the managerial field may be differentiated still further as follows:—

(i) Relationship between the master and crew

The Merchant Shipping Act 1970 brought into effect the first major change for many years in the regulations relating to the employment of seamen. Part of the Act and many of the regulations made thereunder came into force on Jan. 1, 1973. On that date a great deal of earlier legislation was repealed and since then other parts of the Act have become effective. Section 1 of the Act provides that, with certain exceptions, an agreement in writing shall be made between each person employed in the ship and the person employing him, i.e. a contract of employment exists. It is no longer necessary for a mercantile marine superintendent or proper officer to be present at the time of signing on or discharge of the seaman, hence it frequently befalls the master to ensure that the correct procedures are complied with. Since a contract of employment exists with its associated contractual clauses it is the duty of the master to ensure that such clauses are adhered to.

The Merchant Shipping Act 1970 deals with the engagement and discharge of crews, seamen left behind abroad, the payment of a seaman's wages, the relief and repatriation of seamen left behind, deceased seamen, documentation, reports and returns. Separate statutory regulations cover these separate occurrences and it is very important that the master is fully conversant with such regulations. In most cases it is the master, acting on behalf of his employer, who is the responsible person.

A list of crew must be kept by the owner at an address in the United Kingdom and such a list must be up to date, all changes being immediately notified to the employer by the master. In the event of a death occurring on board the next of kin must be notified within three days and a return must be made by the master in addition to him being held responsible for the custody and safe delivery of the deceased seaman's property.

One of the most important documents in the custody of the master is the official log book. Regulations detail the entries to be made in the official log book, the person who should make, sign and witness such entries, the time of making them and provisions for their amendment or cancellation. Offences under the official log book regulations shall, in general, be punishable on summary conviction by a fine.

It is of paramount importance that all documentation required by statute, or otherwise, is accurate since crew agreements, lists of crew, changes in crew agreements and lists of crew, the official log book, returns and reports are admissable in evidence.

(ii) Port health and Customs

The master of a ship arriving from a foreign port is required to notify the port health authority of the district which he is about to enter as to the condition of the crew and passengers on board prior to arrival. On the basis of information received the port health authority may grant the vessel free pratique. Where the master has to notify an infectious disease, etc., or is directed to by the port health authority, he must complete and sign a Maritime Declaration of Health. Under such circumstances only the pilot, a Customs officer or an immigration officer may board or leave the vessel until pratique has been granted.

On arrival in port the ship must be reported in at the Customs House within a specified period. The procedure, in general, is similar at ports throughout the world although certain countries require more detailed information, additional copies, etc., and failure on the part of the master to supply the correct documents may lead to the ship being delayed and to incur heavy penalties.

In the United Kingdom the master may appoint an agent to make a report and obtain clearance outwards of any ship of which he is master. In signing the authorisation the master accepts responsibility for the agent's acts.

Customs formalities must be strictly complied with and it is the responsibility of the master to see that the vessel is rummaged; any high-duty ship's stores placed under seal are the master's responsibility.

(iii) Contracts of affreightment

Where a vessel is under a charter-party, whether it be a voyage, time or demise charter, it is essential for the master of the ship to have a copy of the charter-party since he is responsible for ensuring that the terms of the contract are complied with. Not only does he have to make sure that the shipowner or carrier's obligations under the charter-party are carried out but also those of the charterer. Without his copy he would be unable to comply with those clauses which are of his direct concern, i.e. the time and place of handing in Notice of Readiness, his ability to check the laytime, demurrage and despatch. Masters are required to have a comprehensive knowledge of all the major clauses in charter-parties. In the case of time charters the master frequently acts as the owner's representative at "on" and "off" surveys.

Bills of lading frequently have to be signed by the master and he is required to be fully conversant with the separate entries made on the face of the bill besides a general knowledge of the separate clauses forming the contract of carriage. Some shipping companies instruct their masters to give written authorisation to their agents when the latter are required to sign bills of lading on their behalf.

Should the ship and/or cargo become damaged due to circumstances beyond the control of the master it is his duty to "note protest" before breaking bulk. The "noting of protest" is essential on the Continent where damage is feared and there may be a claim for General Average but it is not a legal necessity in the United Kingdom.

The master is responsible for ensuring the safe loading, stowage, carriage and discharge of the cargo. Although much of this work is delegated to his officers he is, nevertheless, held responsible for any mishaps. At times he may be enticed to accept a letter of indemnity from the shipper of the cargo in exchange for the signing of clean bills of lading. This is a practice fraught with danger since should a master sign clean bills, knowing them to be "foul", he is committing a fraudulent act, conniving with the shipper to deceive an innocent consignee.

(iv) Marine Insurance and General Average

Although there are no legal requirements for a shipowner to insure his ship the majority however are insured. It is unlikely that the master will ever see the policy but nevertheless it is essential for him to have a knowledge of the main clauses embodied in it. It has been said, on occasions, that the master should act in such a manner as though the ship was uninsured.

Implied and expressed warranties must, of course, be strictly complied with, a breach of warranty voiding the policy. Should a breach occur it is essential that the master immediately informs his owners so that additional cover, if necessary, may be arranged. Can a vessel tow, be towed etc.? In the event of an accident the ship may have to put into a port of refuge—masters should be aware of the Tender Clause in the marine insurance policy and thus act in their owners' best interests.

In the event of an accident, fire, etc., there may be a claim for General Average and it is the responsibility of the master to notify his owners and agents at port of discharge that such an act occurred, the extent, as far as is known, of any General Average loss, expenditure or sacrifice incurred so that General Average may be declared at the port(s) of discharge and the appropriate General Average deposit or bond collected before the cargo is released to the consignee.

Modern systems of communications allow a master to maintain close contact with his owners, to obtain advice and instructions, but there are occasions where the master must personally take action on his own account, possibly acting as an "agent of necessity". On very rare occasions the master may have to raise money so as to settle disbursements and continue the voyage, thus requiring him to pledge the ship and/or cargo to raise funds.

(v) Salvage

In the event of an accident involving the ship in a salvage claim it is the duty of the master to ensure that he safeguards his owner's interests at all times. Communication may not always be possible under such circumstances and the master, by taking the appropriate action, by keeping detailed records of events subsequent to and during the salvage operation, may be able to keep the salvage award to a minimum. The master should be conversant with Lloyd's Salvage Agreement and the important clauses contained therein, in addition to the general principles of salvage.

The converse may also be true and the opportunity of salving another vessel may arise. Even though he may have the authority of his owners to carry out such an operation its success or otherwise will depend on the skill of the master. Numerous points will have to be carefully examined before such an exercise is put into effect.

(vi) Pollution

Pollution may take various forms and is of major significance. The greatest fear is that of oil pollution though other forms, sewage, etc., are just as hazardous. In the event of an oil spillage the owner and master may be heavily fined.

Oil records detailing the loading, discharge, transference, etc., of oil, oily water, etc., must be kept and the failure on the part of the master to maintain such detailed records is an offence liable to a fine. In addition to the statutory penalties masters may find themselves summarily dismissed should they personally be found to have been negligent.

Many countries, noticeably the United States of America, have strict pollution laws which include the discharge of untreated sewage, etc., into harbours. It is the duty of masters to ensure that local regulations in respect of pollution are strictly adhered to. Vessels carrying over 2,000 tonnes of cargo oil are required to have a certificate of insurance on board, kept in the custody of the master, and production of this certificate will be required before the vessel is allowed outwards clearance.

(2) The Safety Officer

The master has overall responsibility for all aspects of safety on board ship though he may delegate certain responsibilities to his officers.

There are numerous Statutory Regulations and "M" Notices in respect of shipboard safety. The word "safety" has very wide connotations and since the ship is a potentially dangerous piece of equipment of which the master is in charge his responsibilities may be very wide. "Safety" may be considered under a number of different headings of which the following are a few:—

(i) Safety on board ship

The safety of the crew and passengers must be ensured at all times and nowadays a large number of ships have "safety committees", composed of crew members, to ensure that the regulations, "M" Notices, etc., are complied with. The working conditions of seamen are frequently of a hazardous nature and despite the many precautions that are taken accidents still occur. The only way to instill safety into crew members is to bring to their notice the hazards to which they are exposed since many of the accidents that do occur may have been avoided by the exercise of ordinary and reasonable care.

Where an accident occurs due to a breach of a statutory duty there is practically no defence to a claim for damages and the shipowner may have to meet heavy claims for loss of life and personal injury resulting from such accidents. It is essential that the master brings to the attention of his officers and crew the various publications in respect of safety of which the following are a few:—

Factory Act, Health and Safety at Work Act
Code of Safe Working Practice for the Safety of Merchant Seamen
Tanker Safety Code
Code of Safe Practice for Bulk Cargoes
Dangerous Goods Code
"M" Notices—re safety, etc.

The safety of shore personnel, shore workmen, passengers and other parties is very much the concern of the master and the ship's officers since they require particular care owing to their inexperience and ignorance of shipboard conditions.

Stringent regulations apply in respect of lifesaving and fire-fighting appliances and valid safety certificates must be carried on board showing that the ship complies with the statutory regulations.

Muster regulations require the master of every ship to maintain a muster list showing emergency stations of each crew member, the duties assigned to him in the event of an emergency and the signals calling the crew to emergency stations. They also provide for the mustering and training of crew members in their emergency duties and for the master to appoint emergency stations for passengers. Crew musters must take place at certain times and heavy penalties may be imposed where there is a breach of the regulations.

(ii) Health and welfare

The health and welfare of the crew are of paramount importance and it is the duty of the master, together with a responsible member of the catering department, to regularly inspect the supplies of food and water provided for the crew and enter the result of such an inspection in the official log book.

Where a doctor is not employed on board the master must make sure that any medical attention on board the ship is given by a competent person appointed by him for that purpose. Ships must have on board the latest edition of the Ship Captain's Medical Guide, together with medical stores and medicines in accordance with the regulations.

(iii) Cargoes

Ships may carry a wide variety of cargoes, some of which may be of a hazardous nature. Certain ships are built with specific hazardous cargoes in mind, i.e. LPG's, LNG's, tankers, chemical carriers, etc. Such ships must not only be specifically constructed to carry such cargoes but the officers and crew must also be specially trained in the carriage of these cargoes, the prevention of contamination of such cargoes and the environmental hazards to which they may be exposed. The carriage of dangerous goods is governed by the Merchant Shipping Acts and subsequent regulations and the master may refuse to ship any package which he suspects contains dangerous goods. Dangerous goods which have been sent on board unmarked and without notice may be thrown overboard without the master being subject to any civil or criminal liability.

Certain cargoes, by their very nature, are likely to shift and the appropriate precautions must be taken to prevent such a shift taking place. Ships carrying grain are required to comply with special loading arrangements and such arrangements should ensure that in the event of the cargo shifting the ship remains perfectly seaworthy.

Failure to load a ship in a proper manner may not only give rise to a ship which is unstable but may also impose serious stresses on the hull structure ultimately resulting in failure of the "ship girder". Stability, strength (shearing stresses and bending moments) are all within the scope of the master's responsibilities. Bulk carriers are especially susceptible to high shearing stresses and bending moments, not only in the seagoing condition but during the loading and discharging operation. A ship has been known to break in two due to following an incorrect sequence of discharge and as a result the master was held responsible. Failure to comply with the minimum stability requirements is an infringement of the Load Line Rules.

(iv) Loading of ships

The sending to sea of a ship in an overloaded condition is an infringement of the Load Line Act and the master of a ship who takes the ship to sea when it is overloaded shall be guilty of an offence. Any ship which is overloaded may be detained until such time as she ceases to be so loaded. Failure to keep the ship marked in accordance with the regulations is an offence and a valid Load Line Certificate must be framed and posted up in some conspicuous place on board the ship. Details relating to the deck line and load lines, particulars of freeboard, etc., prior to proceeding to sea must be entered in the official log book and a notice showing such particulars posted in some conspicuous place on board and kept so posted whilst the ship is at sea.

Overloading of a ship is not only an infringement of the Load Line Act but since the ship may be said to be in an unsafe or unseaworthy condition then this may affect her classification with a society and her cover under a marine insurance policy.

(v) *Unseaworthy ship*

A master who knowingly takes a ship to sea in an unseaworthy condition will be guilty of an offence unless he can show that such an action was justifiable.

Seaworthiness not only relates to structural strength but includes equipment, loading and manning. Manning scales are laid down for merchant ships and the regulations require ships to carry a specified number of qualified officers of any description, qualified doctors and qualified cooks and a specified number of other qualified seamen. Different provisions may be made for different descriptions of ships or for ships of the same description but in different circumstances, e.g., different "trading areas".

(vi) *Seamanship and navigation*

It is the master's responsibility to ensure the safe navigation of the ship, that the courses laid off on the chart are safe, that his officers are conversant with the course of action he is taking, that, when appropriate, traffic separation schemes are strictly adhered to, etc. It is necessary for him to have a sound knowledge of meteorology and weather routeing so that he may select the safest and most economical route bearing in mind the prevailing climatic and weather conditions. Owners may advise but cannot direct a master to follow any particular route and the master is solely responsible for ensuring a safe, speedy and economic passage between ports.

In adverse weather conditions, i.e. high seas, gale force winds, etc., the handling of the ship is in the hands of the master. Various options will be open to him, e.g., reducing speed, altering course, etc., but the responsibility for the safe arrival of the ship at her destination lies with the master. Proceeding at full speed in adverse weather conditions may not only damage the ship and cargo but give rise to delays. Such delays may give effect to a subsequent loss of trade, e.g., failing to arrive at a port by the cancelling date in a charter-party.

Certain cargoes of a perishable nature require careful attention to ventilation and consideration must be given to a route which, though not necessarily the shortest, will however ensure the cargo arrives in a sound condition.

(3) The Law Officer

The master of a ship may be said to be the chief law officer on board. It is up to him to ensure that a high standard of discipline is maintained at all times.

Orders must be given and obeyed if a ship is to operate safely and efficiently. Wilful or repeated refusal to comply with reasonable orders or other anti-social behaviour must be expected to have certain consequences. In any emergency the master, officers and petty officers are entitled to look for immediate and unquestioning obedience of orders. There can be no exception to this rule.

In the early 19th century acts of indiscipline such as insubordination, desertion and drunkeness aroused the concern of the Government and in 1850 legislation was introduced with the aim of improving standards of behaviour and discipline. Existing sanctions were strengthened and statutory penalties imposed for a number of offences, including endangering life and the continued disobedience of lawful commands. Masters were empowered to impose monetary fines for the less serious contractual and disciplinary infringements. The Merchant Shipping Act 1894 provided for the less serious offences to be dealt with on board the ship by the master. Six standard offences were approved which applied to non-certificated officers and ratings and were included in every crew agreement signed by a seaman when he joined a ship. The powers for the master to impose penalties for indiscipline were considered essential in those days because ships were away from home for much longer periods than they are today and there was frequently a lack of communication between ship and shore, also conditions on board frequently left much to be desired, e.g., cramped working, living and sleeping conditions.

In 1966 there was a seamen's strike and a Court of Inquiry was appointed to consider amongst other things the terms and conditions of service of seamen. The report of the Court accepted that a special disciplinary regime was necessary at sea and it recommended the retention of certain statutory criminal penalties and the master's powers to impose fines. These recommendations were embodied in the Act of 1970 and as well as providing penalties for the more serious offences also provided for certain offences to be dealt with on board ship by a fining procedure. Sections of the Act also provide for inquiries and investigations into incompetence, misconduct, etc., and for the disqualification of certificated officers and seamen.

In 1974 a Working Group was appointed to review and to make recommendations with respect to disciplinary requirements on board merchant ships with particular reference to the framework of authority required in modern conditions in the interests of safety, good shipboard relations and effective operation.

The principal recommendations were that the present system of shipboard fines should be abolished and a new system of discipline be instituted, similar to those recommended under the ACAS Code of Disciplinary Practice, consisting of informal warnings, recorded warnings, reprimands and final dismissal from the ship and action ashore by a disciplinary committee. Persistent or serious offenders could be excluded from employment within the industry and masters would be provided with wider powers of discharge abroad with a view to the repatriation of serious offenders.

A Code of Conduct for the Merchant Navy would be published and a clause inserted in the crew agreement that a seaman on signing the crew agreement would agree to comply with the Code of Conduct for the time being in force.

On Jan. 1, 1979, a Code of Conduct for the Merchant Navy, published by the National Maritime Board for use on board ships subject to NMB conditions, was incorporated into the contractual clauses of the crew agreement and each seaman on signing the crew agreement thereby agreed to comply with this Code. An additional clause in the crew agreement stipulated that the master's powers to impose fines would not apply to any seaman employed under such an agreement.

It is hoped that in the 1980s a Code of Conduct will be published and incorporated into all crew agreements. At the moment, for those seamen not sailing under NMB crew agreements, the master's power to fine a seaman when in breach of the disciplinary regulations remain.

The Code of Conduct contains a paragraph which sets out a number of acts of indiscipline, any of which, if proved to the reasonable satisfaction of the master, may lead to dismissal from the ship either immediately or at the end of the voyage, in addition to any legal action which may be taken.

Prosecution

Where a seafarer is in breach of the criminal law or certain sections of the Merchant Shipping Act 1970 it is possible for the seafarer to be referred for prosecution ashore. The decision to prosecute will normally lie with the Department of Trade or company.

Master's powers of arrest

The master of any ship registered in the United Kingdom may cause any person on board the ship to be put under restraint if and for so long as it appears necessary to him in the interests of safety or for the preservation of good order or discipline on board the ship.

Although the responsibilities of the master appear very onerous the majority of merchant ships are, however, manned by well qualified and competent officers and ratings. He is therefore able to delegate certain of his responsibilities in the sound knowledge that his orders will be promptly and efficiently carried out.

The ultimate responsibility for the smooth and efficient running of the ship, the safety of personnel on board, the carriage of its cargo, does, however, still lie with the master and he is the one person who will have to answer to his employers, the Courts, etc., in the event of any mishaps occurring.

CHAPTER 12

ADMIRALTY JURISDICTION

1. Introductory

Jurisdiction is the right and power of a Court to entertain proceedings between litigants. Most Courts are subject to restrictions—as to the subject-matter of the case, as to the nationality or domicile of the parties, as to the place where the dispute arose, the amount at issue and many other matters. One aspect of this is of particular significance to maritime claims. As a general proposition, it can be said that Courts will require a close relationship between the claim and the place where the Court is operating: put simply, English Courts generally restrict themselves to English cases.

Admiralty jurisdiction provides an exception to this general rule. From ancient times the Court of the Lord High Admiral asserted the right to hear and decide cases arising outside England, outside English territorial waters, on the high seas, even cases relating to foreign ships. The successor to the Court of the Lord High Admiral is the Admiralty Court, now a special Court within the Queen's Bench Division of the Supreme Court of Judicature, the High Court, and its jurisdiction is described in sections 20-24 of the Supreme Court Act 1981.

First, section 20(1) of the Act sets out, in detail, the particular claims which might be made in respect of a ship or aircraft. Any claim must be brought within one of the 18 categories there set out. Second, the jurisdiction must be appropriately invoked. Courts cannot hear cases unless the parties are properly brought before it. In the ordinary way, that means that the person against whom the claim is brought, or his assets, or preferably both, be within reach of the mechanisms available to the Court to achieve its ends. The normal procedure is called *in personam* procedure. It depends upon serving process upon an individual. It follows that that individual must, in general, be within the effective territorial jurisdiction of the Court in question. To this ordinary way of proceeding in Admiralty we must add an *in rem* procedure: a way of taking action not against an individual but against a piece of property—typically a ship—which is within the reach of the Court.

2. Claims under the Supreme Court Act 1981, section 20(1)

The Act lists the claims in 18 lettered paragraphs, (a) to (s). They are set out below, interspersed, where necessary, with notes of explanation. Most categories are, however, clear in their meaning and application.

(a) any claim to the possession or ownership of a ship or to the ownership of any share therein;

(b) any question arising between the co-owners of a ship as to possession, employment or earnings of that ship;

(c) any claim in respect of a mortgage of or charge on a ship or any share therein.

These three paragraphs cover property claims about ships. The Admiralty Court may hear such claims even where the vessel is foreign registered and foreign owned, though in such case it may exercise its general discretion not to hear a suit that is more conveniently determined elsewhere.

(d) any claim for damage received by a ship;

(e) any claim for damage done by a ship.

Damage suffered by or caused by a ship primarily covers collisions. However, it will also cover damage caused to other property, such as port installations or even oyster-beds, and there is no requirement that the damage be caused by direct physical contact. However, there must be damage, as against loss, and, although the point has not been finally decided, it would seem that claims under contracts for indemnity are not properly brought under either of these two paragraphs. Similarly, although damage done to cargo in a collision is correctly put under para. (e) if the claim is made by the cargo owners against the non-carrying ship, any claim against the carrying ship, being governed by the contract of affreightment, is best classified under (h) below. Oil pollution damage is included by virtue of the Merchant Shipping (Oil Pollution) Act 1971, section 13(1).

(f) any claim for loss of life or personal injury sustained in consequence of any defect in a ship or in her apparel or equipment, or in consequence of the wrongful act, neglect or default of (i) the owners, charterers or persons in possession or control of a ship; or (ii) the master or crew of a ship or of any other person for whose wrongful acts, neglects or defaults the owners, charterers, or persons in possession or control of a ship are responsible, being an act, neglect or default in the navigation or management of the ship, in the loading, carriage or discharge of goods on, in or from the ship or in the embarkation, carriage or disembarkation of persons on, in or from the ship.

This paragraph needs little explanation. Personal injury claims are to be placed in this category even where the claim is based upon a breach of contract, so claims by passengers on their tickets would be included. On the other hand, statutory indemnity or pension entitlements seem to be excluded.

(g) any claim for loss of or damage to goods carried in a ship;

(h) any claim arising out of any agreement relating to the carriage of goods in a ship or to the use or hire of a ship.

These two paragraphs are designed primarily to cover carriage of goods claims. Whether the contract of carriage is only that evidenced by a bill of lading or is contained in a charter-party, whether the claim is for loss or damage, or for some other disaster, all can be brought within these two headings. The second part of para. (h) has caused some discussion, however. The words are to be understood to mean what they say and "agreement relating . . . to the use or hire of a ship" is wide enough to cover a contract of towage under the United Kingdom Standard Towage Conditions, and a standing tug supply contract between two tug owners, and therefore sufficient to ground a claim against the owners of the assisted vessel for indemnity in respect of the loss of a tug so supplied and in respect of liabilities to dependents of deceased crew members (*The Conoco Britannia* [1972] 2 Q.B. 543).

(j) any claim in the nature of salvage (including any claim arising by virtue of the application, by or under section fifty-one of the Civil Aviation Act 1949, of the law relating to salvage to aircraft and their apparel and cargo).

Salvage is dealt with later.

(k) any claim in the nature of towage in respect of a ship or an aircraft;

(l) any claim in the nature of pilotage in respect of a ship or an aircraft;

(m) any claim in respect of goods or materials supplied to a ship for her operation or maintenance;

(n) any claim in respect of the construction, repair or equipment of a ship or dock charges or dues;

(o) any claim by a master or member of the crew of a ship for wages (including any sum allotted out of wages or adjusted by a superintendent to be due by way of wages);

(p) any claim by a master, shipper, charterer or agent in respect of disbursements made on account of a ship.

Disbursements are items of expenditure made in respect of a ship's running costs by the master or other agent of the owner. By maritime law the making of such payments gives a right to reimbursement.

(q) any claim arising out of an act which is or is claimed to be a general average act.

General Average is a system whereby the costs of any sacrifice or expenditure made or incurred for the common safety, in order to preserve the maritime adventure from danger, is rateably shared among the interests which benefit. That is, cargo owner, shipowner and, if there be a difference, the person entitled to receive freight. Thus a General Average act may give rise to a number of claims for contribution between, essentially, cargo owner and shipowner.

(r)   any claim arising out of bottomry.

Bottomry is a nearly obsolete method of securing an advance upon a ship.

(s)   any claim for the forfeiture or condemnation of a ship or of goods which are being or have been carried, or have been attempted to be carried, in a ship, or for the restoration of a ship or any such goods after seizure, or for droits of Admiralty.

A claimant who is unable to get the claim in question within one of the above categories cannot proceed in Admiralty unless it is possible to prove that the claim in question existed before the statute as an item of Admiralty jurisdiction. Such rights are preserved, though their practical significance is very low.

3. In personam jurisdiction

In personam procedure is the ordinary method of invoking the jurisdiction of the High Court. The Supreme Court Act 1981, in section 21, declares that this procedure is available in respect of the special Admiralty Court claims enumerated in section 20 of the Act (and set out in the last section).

The principle of *in personam* proceedings is simple. A claim is made by one person, the plaintiff, against another, the defendant. The plaintiff obtains a writ to commence the action and serves it upon the defendant. This he may do anywhere within the geographical jurisdiction of the Court, that is, for our purposes, within England and Wales. There is no requirement that the defendant be ordinarily resident in the country, that he be domiciled (that is, permanently resident) still less that he be a British National. A foreign defendant, passing through Heathrow Airport on vacation may, if the plaintiff is speedy and lucky enough, be served.

Most defendants in maritime claims are companies. A company is regarded as within the geographical jurisdiction if it carries on business here. It does not need to be registered in the United Kingdom. It does not even need to own or occupy an office here. It can be enough that the business it does is regularly carried on by a particular agent with an office here (see *The World Harmony, Konstantinidis* v. *World Tankers Corporation Inc.* [1965] 2 All E.R. 139).

Of course, there is often very little point in beginning proceedings against defendants who have little or no real connection with the country. The purpose of legal action is usually to get financial satisfaction and, unless there are assets available to meet the claim if successful, there is little to be gained by the proceedings. However, assets there may be, and the Court is equipped to ensure that a foreign defendant, when proceedings have begun, does not frustrate the purpose of the action by removing his assets from the reach of the Court.

If the defendant cannot be found in the jurisdiction, the plaintiff may ask the Court for leave to serve his writ outside the jurisdiction. This is a matter for the Court's discretion, but there are established occasions when such leave will normally be granted. These are to be found in the regulations governing High Court procedure, the Rules of the Supreme Court, Order 11, Rule 1. Many of those occasions are unlikely to be significant in litigation concerning ships and the sea. Those that may be are:

1. Where the defendant, though temporarily absent, is domiciled or ordinarily resident in the country.
2. Where the claim concerns a contract made within the jurisdiction: in such a case much of the law governing that contract may be English.
3. Where the contract was made through the agency of an agent resident or trading within the jurisdiction. This has particular significance for British shipbrokers. The contracts they negotiate and conclude will usually fall into this category, so that their foreign principals will be subject to service out.
4. Where the claim concerns a contract which, by its express terms or by implication, is governed by English law.
5. Where the claim relates to a contract allegedly broken within the jurisdiction.
6. Where the claim relates to a tort committed here.
7. Where service of a person outside the jurisdiction is necessary in respect of proceedings against a defendant within the jurisdiction.

In respect of certain maritime claims, these general rules relating to service of defendants actually within the jurisdiction and to permitted service outside the jurisdiction, are subject to further restrictions. The claims in question are collision claims. They are specifically defined by section 22 of the Supreme Court Act 1981 as follows:

". . . any claim for damages, loss of life or personal injury arising out of—
(a) a collision between ships; or

> (b) the carrying out of, or omission to carry out, a manoeuvre in the case of one or more of two or more ships; or
>
> (c) non-compliance, in the case of one or more of two or more ships, with the collision regulations".

The extra requirements added by section 22 in respect of collision proceedings are that one of the following conditions be satisfied:

> (a) the defendant has his habitual residence or a place of business within England and Wales; or
>
> (b) the cause of action arose within inland waters of England and Wales or within the limits of a port of England and Wales; or
>
> (c) an action arising out of the same incident or series of incidents is proceeding in the Court or has been heard and determined in the Court.

Further, if proceedings have been previously commenced in a Court *outside* England and Wales, the English Court must not proceed until such proceedings have been disposed of. Proceedings begun on the same day as English proceedings are not "previously" brought (see *The World Harmony*, referred to above).

The limits and restrictions surrounding the use of *in personam* procedure are all subject to one massive qualification. The parties to the proceedings, plaintiff and defendant, may within very broad limits agree to accept the jurisdiction of the Court. A foreign defendant may submit to the jurisdiction of the Court: he may do this expressly; or impliedly, by entering an appearance unconditionally to the proceedings. This overriding right to submit to the jurisdiction also covers the special restrictions contained in section 22 of the Supreme Court Act 1981.

In practice, service by a defendant is generally accepted by the defendant's solicitor. Such acceptance may even be made without prejudice to the defendant's right to challenge the jurisdiction of the Court at a later stage. In practice it is rare for it to be necessary to activate Order 11 and seek leave to serve out of the jurisidction. But the practice depends upon agreement.

4. In rem jurisdiction

In personam proceedings are not difficult to understand. The plaintiff takes action against the defendant by serving process upon his person. Proceedings *in rem* begin with process being served upon a *thing* (Latin: *res*), typically a ship. Historically, these proceedings, peculiar to Admiralty jurisdiction, are linked with another peculiar Admiralty institution, the maritime lien. A lien is a right to hold the property of another as security for something owed, a debt or damages. An example from the general law is a hotel-keeper's lien, whereby the proprietor of a hotel may impound the suitcases of a guest until the bill is paid. However, *in rem* proceedings are now largely separated from the maritime lien, and indeed the law of maritime liens has been extended and altered by the statute which governs Admiralty procedure.

This historical connection has added to a confusion often found in discussing *in rem* proceedings. If a writ is being served on a ship, it appears that legal action is actually being taken against a thing rather than against a person. If there is also a lien, whereby, in some circumstances, the ship may be held against payment of the amount owed even though it is presently owned by someone other than the person responsible for the debt or liability, that impression is confirmed. Add to that the common shorthand used, especially in collision actions, whereby the vessel is personified—"The *Andreas B.* collided with the *Basingstoke Trader;* the *Andreas B.* was not keeping proper look-out and was therefore held liable"—and the confusion is complete. However, although legal difficulties may arise, it is important to emphasize that the ship, the *res*, is not being made liable, is not being proceeded against, it is the owner or other responsible person who is defendant. Indeed, there is judicial authority for the view that once the defendant to proceedings *in rem* enters an appearance, the proceedings are converted into *in personam* proceedings against him (see *The Conoco Britannia* [1972] 2 All E.R. 238, at p. 244).

In rem proceedings are available in respect of all the claims enumerated in section 20 of the Supreme Court Act 1981, which were set out and described in section 2 above. With the exception of claims within paras. (a), (b), (c) and (s) of section 20, which are concerned with disputes relating to the ownership of ships or other property, the writ may be issued either against the ship or other property at issue in the dispute or against another ship (if the dispute refers, as is most common, to a ship) "beneficially owned" by the defendant at the time the action is brought. The advantages of this "sister ship" procedure are obvious. It was clearly not thought necessary to extend that advantage to cases where the very purpose of the litigation was to decide who was entitled to the ship in dispute.

A writ *in rem* does not name the defendants to the action. It is addressed to the "owners and other persons interested in" the ship in respect of which it is issued. The writ operates as notice of the existence of the claim and that notice is made effective by service of the writ. The mechanics of service are that the writ, and later a copy, is affixed to some prominent part of the superstructure of the ship in question. Similar action is taken if the property named is not a ship. Service of the writ is not an arrest: an arrest is effected by a warrant of arrest, which may be applied for at any time after issue of the writ, even before the writ has been served. A warrant of arrest is executed by the Admiralty Marshal, an officer of the Court. When a vessel has been arrested, she may not be interfered with. Such interference amounts to a contempt of Court and may lead to imprisonment.

In sister ship proceedings or in any proceedings where there is no maritime lien (liens, maritime and statutory, will be discussed below) a warrant for arrest must be accompanied by affidavits to the effect that the defendant to the action was in possession or control, or owned, the ship involved in the claim when the claim arose and was beneficial owner of the ship against which the writ was issued at the date the writ was issued. This is intended to ensure that the vessel proceeded against is one to which a valid lien attaches.

The main purpose of the *in rem* procedure is to establish a fund of accessible assets to satisfy the claim, if the claim proves successful. Such a fund may be created by the ship itself. From the plaintiff's point of view, however, whether the ship or some other source of wealth is used makes no difference. The normal practice is to replace the ship with bail: the claim is often of much less value than that represented by the vessel, and, in any case, by replacing his ship with bonds promising money, the defendant obtains the economic benefit of the use of his ship.

Bail is formal binding undertaking to meet the claim, up to a maximum amount specified in the bail bond. Unless the right to limit liability does not arise, or is disputed, the amount of bail will be the limitation value of the ship. (Limitation proceedings are considered below.) If the limitation fund is not appropriate, then the bond must be as great as the claim. In practice, this is usually a matter for negotiation and agreement between the parties.

If bail is to replace arrest, the defendant's solicitor will accept service of the writ and the warrant of arrest and make a written undertaking to enter an appearance in the action and to put in bail. That undertaking is binding upon him. If he fails in either respect he is guilty of contempt of Court and may be committed to prison. On the undertaking being given, there is no need to execute the warrant of arrest and, if by chance the vessel has already been arrested, it will be freed. The undertaking, however, cannot be withdrawn.

Bail is generally effected through insurance or other interests.

5. Public ships

The *in rem* procedure is not available against vessels owned by the Crown. *In personam* proceedings are possible under the Crown Proceedings Act 1947. The distinction reflects a view as to whether, historically, the Monarch was subject to legal process.

Similar limitations apply to foreign government-owned ships. In the 19th century the accepted view was that the Court could not take any sort of jurisdiction over vessels owned by foreign governments, even when they were engaged on ordinary commercial adventures—such as that of a cross-channel ferry. More recently, in *The Philippine Admiral* (*Owners*) v. *Wallem Shipping* (*Hong Kong*) *Ltd.* [1976] 2 W.L.R. 214, the Court has decided that the general immunity from proceedings only applies to public, or government-owned, ships when used for public purposes. So if, as is common in today's world of national shipping lines and State carrying corporations, a government-owned ship trades commercially, proceedings may be brought against that government or government agency in the English Admiralty Court. However, the restriction in respect of the action *in rem* still seems to stand. A foreign sovereign may not be sued by action *in rem*.

In practice these problems are less real than apparent, for two reasons. First, many State-controlled agencies are, upon close examination, sufficiently distant from the foreign government to be regarded as distinct from it. Second, and more important, a foreign State agency may, and commonly does, voluntarily submit to the jurisdiction of the Admiralty Court, even in proceedings *in rem*.

6. Liens, maritime and statutory

A lien arises when some person with a claim against another is able to take possession of that other person's property and use that possession as security against payment. Sometimes the lien-holder has the legal right to obtain possession but this right must generally be exercised by legal procedure. Sometimes, too, the lien-holder may realise his security and sell the property he holds in order to extract what is owed to him.

Maritime liens are ancient devices and are liens of a highly efficient variety. A holder of a maritime lien may use *in rem* procedure to obtain possession of the property in question and has the ultimate right, after successful proceedings, to sell the goods to obtain his debt. Maritime liens, strictly so-called, come into existence in five sets of circumstances:

1. The holder of a bottomry bond has a maritime lien on ship and cargo for repayment of his loan. Bottomry bonds are now obsolete: they were a method whereby the master of a ship might pledge hull and cargo for advances for necessaries.

2. The master of a ship has a lien on the ship in respect of his proper disbursements for necessaries. Other agents of the shipowner, who have laid out money by way of disbursements for necessaries, although they have a good legal claim against the owner, have no maritime lien.

3. The master and crew of a ship have a maritime lien over the ship in respect of their unpaid wages.

4. A claimant in respect of damage done by a ship, not including oil pollution damage for which liability is imposed by statute, has a lien over the ship that caused the damage for the damages suffered.

5. The provider of salvage services has a maritime lien over any property salved, ship or cargo, for his salvage reward, including any sum due for life salvage.

Of the five, the last two have very much greater practical importance than the first three.

A maritime lien is created by the event in question: the collision, the rendering of salvage services, the disbursement. It is said to create a right in the ship or other property from that moment. That right is incomplete—or inchoate, as the cases have it—and is completed by the institution of proceedings *in rem*. However, it still exists, incomplete or not. Its existence, therefore, is not affected by dealings in the property between the happening of the event and the commencement of proceedings. In the leading case on this, *The Bold Buccleugh* (1851) 7 Moo. P.C. 267, a purchaser of a vessel with no knowledge that it had been involved in a collision before he had bought it was held liable in proceedings to enforce the maritime lien. Of course, the vendor of property subject to a maritime lien will, most likely, be in breach of his contract of sale if he made no disclosure, and may be sued for compensation. Again, although the distinction seems to make very little difference, the innocent purchaser is not being made legally liable for the collision. He is simply the owner of a piece of property, one slice of which, in a manner of speaking, really belongs to someone else. He should join the true defendant to the proceedings and have him defend the action.

The lien, however, does *not* arise if the owner of the property in question was never liable at the time of the event in question. So if the services rendered were not, in truth, salvage services, or if the owner of the ship was not legally liable for the losses caused by the collision, because there was no negligence, or because the damage was caused by the malicious act of the master, or by government action when the vessel was under compulsory requisition, the lien never was created; proceedings *in rem* cannot therefore be brought against the owner or any subsequent purchaser.

In olden times, the *in rem* action was only available where there was a maritime lien. Under the Supreme Court Act 1981, as we have seen, the right to proceed *in rem* is available in respect of all claims in the Admiralty Court. The *in rem* procedure is said to create a lien as well, although this is not a true maritime lien.

It is called a *statutory lien* and is brought into existence not by the occurrence in question but by the commencement of proceedings. A statutory lien, therefore, begins with the issue of the writ and cannot be asserted if the ship has been disposed of between the event and that moment. It is not affected, however, by dispositions after the issue of the writ, even if they occur before service of the writ (see *The Monica S.* [1968] P. 741).

7. Limitation of actions

Limitation of actions is that part of the law of procedure which imposes a time-limit on the commencement of actions and suits. For example, in the general law, an action for damages for personal injuries must be commenced by issue of writ within three years of the accrual of the cause of action—in practice, within three years of the injury.

By historical accident, the Admiralty action *in rem* is not subject to the general law of limitation of actions as contained in the Limitation Act 1975. However, there are certain special limitation rules that govern maritime matters.

First, actions to recover seaman's wages are subject to a six-year limitation period.

Much more important, by section 8 of the Maritime Conventions Act 1911, there is a two-year limitation period in respect of any claim, whether the *in rem* or the *in personam* procedure is used:

> ". . . in respect of any damage or loss to another vessel, her cargo or freight, or any property on board her or damages for loss of life or personal injuries suffered by any person on board her, caused by the fault of [the defendant's] vessel, whether that vessel is wholly or partly in fault, or in respect of any salvage services . . .".

The two-year period runs from the date when the damage, loss or injury was caused or from the date when the salvage services were rendered.

This somewhat short limitation period applies, therefore, to salvage claims and to claims for damage caused by a ship to a ship. Personal injury claims and claims for damage to goods are within the rule only in so far as they are claims against the *other* vessel involved in the collision and are not claims against the carrying ship. That would be a claim on the contract of affreightment.

Third, the Hague-Visby Rules impose, as a condition of any liability in the carrier, that proceedings must be commenced within a period of one year from the date upon which the goods were delivered or, if they were not delivered, should have been delivered. This rule is compulsory when the Hague-Visby Rules are compulsory in virtue of the Carriage of Goods by Sea Act 1971.

8. Limitation of liability

A rather peculiar feature of admiralty practice is that defendants in certain cases have a statutory right to limit their liability. This is to be distinguished from a contractual right to limit liability: within broad limitations, any contracting party has the right to restrict his liability by his contract. Contracts for the carriage of goods by sea are a case in point: the conclusion of the history of contractual limitation of liability has been the compulsory adoption of an internationally agreed scheme governing the style and extent of that limitation—the Hague Rules as enacted by the Carriage of Goods by Sea Acts. However, the basis of the limitation is contractual: it is always possible for the carrier to increase his legal liabilities by express agreement.

Statutory limitation is different. If the claim is one to which the legal right applies, the defendant, by appropriate proceedings, may fix the total limit for his liability. The liability may arise from tort or from breach of contract and the agreed terms of any contract are generally irrelevant. If the claim does not reach that statutory limit, it must be met in full. If it exceeds it, the claim is reduced. If there are several claims, they are all reduced proportionately. The right to limit is contained in section 503 of the Merchant Shipping Act 1894, as amended by several subsequent Acts, notably the Merchant Shipping (Liability of Shipowners and Others) Act 1958. In 1976 a new international Convention on limitation of liability was adopted and that Convention now appears in the Merchant Shipping Act 1979: however, that part of the 1979 Act has not yet been brought into force. It is unlikely that it will be brought into force before the Convention has received sufficient support for it to become a binding international agreement. At that point, by international law, the government will be obliged to bring it into effect as part of English law.

The claims subject to limitation are of two basic types. The first type includes claims for loss of life or personal injuries or for loss of or damage to goods, the goods or injured or deceased persons being goods or persons carried on board the vessel subject to limitation. Thus it applies to ordinary cargo claims as well as to personal injury claims made by passengers or crew members. Claims of the second type might be called external claims. These are claims for loss of life, personal injuries, loss of or damage to goods, when the goods or persons are *not* aboard the limiting vessel. Such claims are limitable only if they are based upon one of four types of fault connected with the operation of the ship. These four faults are:

1. A fault in the navigation of the ship.
2. A fault in the management of the ship.
3. A fault in the loading or discharge of cargo of the embarkation or disembarkation of passengers.
4. A fault (of any other sort) by a person aboard the ship.

These categories of fault are generally sufficient to cover the basis of most claims likely to be made "from outside" the limiting vessel. Occasionally there are problems. In *The Tojo Maru* [1972] A.C. 242, the fault of a diver working from a salvage tug was not limitable: he was not aboard the tug and his fault lay neither in the navigation nor in the management of the tug.

Claims subject to limitation may arise from a breach of contract or from a tort. However, they must be claims for loss of or damage to property, or for personal injury or death. Claims for money indemnity, such as for example may arise under a towage contract whereby the owner of the vessel under tow agrees to indemnify the tug owner in respect of damage or expenses suffered or incurred by the tug, are not claims for loss of or damage to property. They are claims for reimbursement of money and may not be limited. (See *The Kirknes* [1957] P. 51). It is possible, by the express terms of a contract, to exclude the right to limit, but this must be done by clear words. In one case the competitors in a yacht race effectively agreed, through the rules governing the race, not to limit liability in respect of claims arising out of collisions during the race (*The Satanita, Clarke* v. *Earl of Dunraven* [1897] A.C. 59).

Limitation is a right that arises primarily in respect of ships. Under the Merchant Shipping (Liability of Shipowners and Others) Act 1958, the definition of ships was expanded so as to include "any structure, whether completed or in the course of completion, launched and intended for use in navigation as a ship or part of a ship." The governing notion remains "use in navigation," which leaves us with problems concerning many maritime structures, especially those concerned with oil exploration and production. To meet this sort of problem, the Merchant Shipping Act 1979 gives the Secretary of State power to specify structures as ships for the purpose of limitation proceedings, amongst other matters. This power has not yet been exercised.

Originally, only the owner of the ship could limit liability. This right was successively extended. Now, by section 3(1) of the Merchant Shipping (Liability of Shipowners and Others) Act 1958, "the charterer or any person interested in or in possession of the ship and in particular any manager or operator" may limit. That same Act also extends the right of limitation to employees, so as to avoid the apparent gap in the system whereby, in the event of a collision or other accident, the plaintiff who sued the crew member actually responsible (rather than his employer who was also legally responsible), would be in a better legal position, at least theoretically. So section 3(2)(a) of the Act permits a "master, member of the crew or servant" similar rights to limit liability.

The right of limitation is lost if the defendant is personally at fault. The words used are "actual fault or privity". "Actual fault" is not difficult to understand. If the case shows that the collision was contributed to by some failing in the owner as well as the crew operating the ship—some failure in maintenance, manning or supply, for example—there is a possibility of actual fault. "Privity" seems to mean knowledge of the circumstances giving rise to the fault in navigation, management, etc., on the ship, and understanding of its significance. Mere failure in supervision is unlikely to be held to be "privity" unless it is so bad as to amount to purposeful "shutting one's eyes". However, the words are capable of many interpretations and some jurisdictions in the world give a very broad meaning to them indeed.

The owner is usually a company and the question therefore arises as to where in the company the actual fault or privity must be located to amount to the actual fault or privity of the corporation itself. The answer seems to be that it depends upon the internal organisation of the particular company. In *The Lady Gwendolen* [1965] P. 294, the failure of the marine superintendent to ensure the master of the ship was fully conversant with the use and limitations of radar systems was the actual fault of a brewing company: he, within the company, had effective charge of the company's extremely small shipowning operation.

When the person seeking limitation is an employee, there can be no room for the operation of the actual fault and privity rule and it does not apply.

Limitation is effected by reference to the ship's registered tonnage. There are two funds. In respect of property claims the fund is expressed as 1,000 gold francs per registered ton. A gold franc is expressed as "65 1/2 milligrams of gold of millesimal fineness 900" and is, for the purposes of English jurisdiction, given a sterling equivalent from time to time. Personal injury claims are made against a larger fund: 3,100 gold francs per ton and there is a "platform tonnage" of 300 tons for this fund. Small vessels may not limit in personal injury claims to less than £39,474. If there are both personal injury and property claims the personal injury claims are taken first against the difference between the two funds (i.e. 2,100 gold francs per ton) and, if the "difference fund" is not sufficient, the balance of the personal injury claims rank proportionately with the property claims in the 1,000 gold francs per ton property fund.

If there is likely to be dispute about limitation, for example on the issue of actual fault or privity, on whether the claim is limitable, upon how many limitable claims there are, the defendant to the action or actions may apply to the Court for a determination of the issue. In these limitation proceedings the defendant to the actions appears as plaintiff. The Court will then proceed to determine the value of the claims and include relevant claims and exclude others and allocate liability within the fund. In many cases, of course, limitation will be disposed of as a matter of agreement between the parties at the time that service is accepted and bail put in.

There are also special limitation provisions relating to claims against harbour authorities and pilotage authorities. Oil spillage is specially dealt with, and the limitation fund is very much larger, under the Merchant Shipping (Oil Pollution) Act 1971.

9. Collision claims and the Both-to-Blame Clause

When collisions occur there may be consequential claims for compensation. Liability in maritime collisions is based upon the same legal principles as liability in land-based collisions: the principles of negligence. A successful claimant must be able to show that the damage was brought about by the failure of some person to behave with *reasonable care with regard to reasonably foreseeable risks* (see *Donoghue* v. *Stevenson* [1932] A.C. 562). If such negligence is found, as is common, in the navigation or operation of the ship, the person negligent will generally be the master or a member of the ship's crew. Such a person remains legally liable but, in so far as his negligence occurred in the course of his employment, the shipowner, as employer, is also held to be legally liable. This is the principle of vicarious liability.

There are internationally accepted standards of good seamanship. Such standards find their legal expression in the Collision Regulations. These rules, governing lights and shapes, steering and sailing and traffic separation schemes, distress signals, etc., are binding upon seafarers and those who break them may be prosecuted or perhaps lose their certificates of competency. Clearly, too, the breach of such rules is good evidence of negligence. Until the passing of the Maritime Conventions Act 1911, it was more than that. By statute, fault was presumed from failure to observe a governing regulation. That is no longer the law: breach of regulation is but one factor perhaps among many (see *The Heranger* (*Owners*) v. *The Diamond* (*Owners*) [1939] A.C. 94).

Such claims in maritime law were subject to the rule of division of loss, long before such a principle was accepted as applicable to land-based claims. Division of loss means that if two vessels are in collision and the collision is found to have been brought about by the fault of both, then the loss suffered by each is divided. Until 1911 each was entitled to claim half its loss from the other. One claim was set off against the other and the balance was enforced against the limitation fund of the appropriate ship. The Maritime Conventions Act 1911 replaced the 50% rule with a fault-based division. Now the Court will allocate liability in accordance with the respective degrees of fault. The process of division is a question of fact for the Court and is not generally subject to appeal. It is therefore hard to be certain what sort of principles, if any, govern the matter.

The same principles apply when the collision involves more than two vessels. So long as they are all at fault, the Court will generally make an apportionment between all of them in terms of their respective proportions of blame—usually expressed in percentages. Clearly the parties can (and often do) agree such proportions, especially where there is no dispute as to liability. The governing practice of the English Courts has been *not* to treat such co-active wrongdoers as "joint tortfeasors". Joint tortfeasors are those who together commit one wrong, or tort. Joint tortfeasors are "jointly and severally" liable: each is wholly responsible for the whole of the damages. However, joint tortfeasors may, under the Law Reform (Married Women and Joint Tortfeasors) Act 1935, claim a contribution from their co-joint tortfeasors. Thus, the English Court of Admiralty will make individual allocations of responsibility to each for part of the loss of the other or others (see *The Panther and the Ericbank* [1957] P. 143).

A cargo owner can suffer loss in a collision. As regards any claim against the owners of the ship upon which his goods were carried, his claim will be governed by his contract of affreightment. That contract will, most likely exclude liability for the damage as being caused by a "peril of the sea"—for collisions are so regarded. There is no obstacle to his suing the other vessel or vessels involved in the collision, however, and since he has no contract with them there can be no contractual exclusion or limitation of liability. However, under English law it is established that such a claim may only be maintained for the proportion of the loss for which such other vessel would be liable by way of apportionment under section 1 of the Maritime Conventions Act 1911. (See *Tongariro (Cargo Owners)* v. *Drumlanrig (Owners)* [1911] A.C. 16.)

This is not the position in the United States of America, where the Courts take the view that where a collision occurs as a result of the fault of two or more vessels, there is joint and several liability between those owners towards cargo claims. So it is possible to maintain proceedings for the full loss against the "outside" shipowner, who will then be able to make whatever claim is appropriate against the carrying shipowner. (*The Beaconsfield* (1894) 158 U.S. 303.) From the carrying shipowner's point of view, this imposes on him a liability which appeared to be covered by the contract of affreightment. To meet this problem, the "both to blame" clause was developed and is used in contracts of affreightment. It provides:

> "If the vessel comes into collision with another ship as a result of the negligence of the other ship and any act, neglect or default of the master, mariner, pilot or the servants of the Carrier in the navigation or in the management of the vessel, the Owner of the goods carried hereunder will indemnify the Carrier against all loss or liability to the other or non-carrying ship or her Owners in so far as such loss or liability represent loss of, or damage to or any claim whatsoever of the Owner of the said goods, paid or payable by the other or non-carrying ship or her Owners to the Owner of the said goods and set off, recouped or recovered by the

other or non-carrying ship or her Owners as part of their claim against the carrying vessel or Carrier. The foregoing provisions shall also apply where the Owners, Operators or those in charge of any ship or ships or objects other than, or in addition to, the colliding ships or objects are at fault in respect to a collision or contact".

The aim of the clause is to ensure that the shipowner is indemnified in respect of any contribution the carrier is obliged to make to another shipowner in respect of loss or damage to the shipper's cargo. The effectiveness of this clause in the United States of America may not be complete.

10. Salvage

The principle of salvage is that those who voluntarily render meritorious service to endangered maritime property, and achieve success, are entitled to a reward commensurate with their merit and success. It is an ancient and, in the general legal context, somewhat unusual idea.

Salvage rewards may be claimed by all those who are involved in the salvage operation: the master, the crew, and the owner of the vessel rendering assistance. The owner is accorded the largest share, on the grounds that it was he who, in economic terms at least, had most at risk.

Salvors must be voluntary: those who are already under a duty to take action cannot claim salvage. The result of this is, first, that those under public duties in this regard generally have to demonstrate that they did more than was required of them, though generalised public duties (such as that placed on all seafarers to answer distress calls) are disregarded. Second, those under contractual duties are in a specially difficult position when it comes to salvage claims. Particularly we must consider members of the crew of the ship in distress and those performing services under a contract, such as a towage contract. The Court views such claims with some cynical disfavour and claimants would have to show that the circumstances were such that their original contractual obligations could be said to have been discharged by events—or, in law, frustrated.

Salvage depends upon success. So salvage rewards are payable from the property saved and the amount reflects the value of what is saved. A complicating factor is the recognition of salvage rewards for life salvage. Life salvors are entitled to a reward, and this entitlement is preserved and enhanced by the Merchant Shipping Act 1894. Life salvors may claim against ship or cargo saved, even if they themselves did not save any such property. Further, life salvage claims have priority and, if there is insufficient property saved, the Secretary of State may make up life salvage rewards from the Mercantile Marine Fund.

Salvage claims are subject to a maritime lien. This lien attaches to maritime property (ship, goods and freight) from the moment the services are rendered. The reward is a charge upon the property saved. Salvage only applies to maritime property (including derelict property—flotsam, jetsam and laggan) and there may be problems with objects found in or about the sea which are neither ship nor cargo. Again, the power under the Merchant Shipping Act 1979 to declare doubtful structures to be ships may be used to solve some of these problems.

In a salvage claim the Court may fix the amount of salvage reward appropriate to each salving interest, individuals and shipowning companies, and allocate responsibility among the owners of the salved property.

Much salvage is carried out professionally. Salvage companies may render their services under whatever contractual arrangements seem good to them. They may hire their tugs and equipment at so much per day, enter into towage contracts or any other appropriate arrangement. Such contracts raise few problems. They may, however, make salvage contracts: they may agree to save the ship or cargo. This they may do for an agreed sum or for an amount to be determined by arbitration. In either case, the Court of Admiralty has an overriding jurisdiction to inquire into such contracts and strike them down if they reveal undue pressure or lack of good faith. Such cases are rare today. Salvage contracts are nowadays generally negotiated at arms-length between professional salvors and well-advised shipping companies. The principle, however, remains.

Contractual salvors often use "open-form" contracting, by the Lloyd's "No cure-No pay" or Open Form. This contract requires that the salvor "use his best endeavours" to salve the property in question, for which he is to receive a sum fixed by arbitration in accordance with the ordinary principles of maritime law applicable to salvage. Thus, by his contract, an open-form salvor is placed in the position of a voluntary salvor.

It is now established that salvors, contractual and voluntary, are under a legal duty to take care in carrying out the salvage. They may, therefore, be sued for negligent salvage (see *The Tojo Maru* [1972] A.C. 242) but voluntary salvors will not be obliged to observe as high a standard of care as professional contractual salvors (see *The St. Blane* [1974] 1 Lloyd's Rep. 557). Salvors, therefore, may sometimes require an indemnity before they undertake the work, particularly if consequential liabilities seem likely to be high: there may, for example, be a risk of oil-spill. Their position is not improved by their present doubtful position on limitation. The 1976 Limitation Convention contains proposals which would give salvors a limitation fund even when they were not working with a ship. This Convention is not yet in force.

CHAPTER 13

OWNERSHIP AND REGISTRATION OF BRITISH SHIPS

1. Registrable ships

Every British ship must be registered under the Merchant Shipping Acts (Merchant Shipping Act 1894, section 2). This provision is less simple than it looks. "Ship" means "every description of vessel used in navigation not propelled by oars" (M.S.A. 1894, section 742). Rowing boats apart, the crucial phrase is "used in navigation". There is first the question of *where* the vessel is used: it must be used in navigable waters. So a pleasure boat on a park lake was not a ship in *Southport Corpn.* v. *Morris* [1893] 1 Q.B. 359. It must be constructed for the purpose of navigation, that is, for travelling over water from one place to another, and not for some other purpose. A floating beacon which looked rather like a ship was not a registrable ship in *Gas Float Whitton No.* 2 [1897] A.C. 337. On the other hand, a vessel remains a ship if, though constructed for use in navigation, it is currently not so used, because, for example, it is temporarily disabled, or being used for some other purpose—storage, for instance—for a short period.

Navigation may occur in a vessel not capable of self-propulsion. The Courts decided in *The Harlow* [1922] P. 175 that a barge fitted with a rudder was a ship and the legislature put the matter beyond doubt by enacting, in the Merchant Shipping Act 1921, that "every description of lighter, barge or like vessel used in navigation in Great Britain, however propelled" should be a ship. This would even include oar-driven lighters, should any still exist, which provides the one example of a registrable British rowed boat. The Merchant Shipping Act 1921 applies only to vessels used in British tidal waters.

The modern problem is that posed by structures and constructions found in or on the sea which may or may not look like ships, may or may not float or may not float all the time, and may or may not move or be moved from place to place. A flying boat was not treated as a ship in *Polpen Shipping* v. *Commercial Union Assurance* [1943] K.B. 167. Flying boats are registered as aircraft. Hovercraft are specially treated under the Hovercraft Act 1968. Finally, to provide for the solution to the apparently endless questions posed by semi-submersible drilling rigs and other such structures, the Merchant Shipping Act 1979, section 41, empowers the Secretary of State to make orders providing that any structure designed or adapted for use at sea is to be treated as a ship for the purpose of the Merchant Shipping Acts and the Prevention of Oil Pollution Act. This power has not yet been exercised.

Not all ships are registrable. Apart from those already implicitly described—vessels other than barges and lighters in British waters propelled by oars and "non-ships"— the obligation to register is subject to exemption. There are three exemptions.

The first two relate to small vessels. Ships not exceeding 15 tons used solely in coastal or river navigation in the United Kingdom or some British possession are exempt, as are undecked vessels not exceeding 30 tons used solely in fishing or coastal trading in Newfoundland or the Gulf of St. Lawrence.

The third exemption is more simple. Her Majesty's ships are not registrable, save that non-naval vessels (for example, Royal Fleet Auxiliary ships) are registrable by analogous procedure established by Order in Council.

For the purpose of registration, the ownership of a ship is divided into 64 equal shares. Multiple ownership of a ship is not common today, but if it exists it must take effect in terms of these 64 shares. A part owner will be the owner of one or more sixty-fourths of a vessel. The shares may not be further subdivided, but one (or more) share(s) may be held by more than one owner, provided that the several owners own the share in common.

2. Nationality

As we have said, every registrable British ship must be British registered. A British ship may be detained (in British waters) and not released until the master has produced a Certificate of Registry to show that it is registered in accordance with the Merchant Shipping Acts.

A British ship is a ship that is wholly owned by British owners. Such owners may, of course, be individual human beings or, much more probably, companies. The rules for identifying their "Britishness" differ depending upon whether we are examining a person or a company.

The Merchant Shipping Act 1894 was intended to provide a code of shipping law which would apply throughout the then British Empire. Several parts of the Act are expressed to apply much more widely than to the United Kingdom and its territorial waters. Registration is within one of those parts. By section 91 of the Merchant Shipping Act 1894 the registration provisions apply throughout Her Majesty's dominions—which phrase includes the British Commonwealth.

The policy of a common maritime law, in certain areas, survived the transformation of the Empire into the Commonwealth and the growth of independence in British possessions. In 1931 the Commonwealth Maritime Committee was set up, representative of the new dominions and had, as part of its constitution, the creation of a common system of registration of ships throughout the Commonwealth. It still exists.

Today, of course, independent Commonwealth countries have the power to pass their own Merchant Shipping Acts: some have done so. In such cases, their own laws clearly apply to their own territories. However, we still have the remnants of imperial ship-registration. Ports of registry, under the British Merchant Shipping Act 1894, exist outside the United Kingdom.

If the shipowner is a human being, he is British if he is a British subject. "British subject" is defined by the British Nationality Act 1948, and, in distinction from "U.K. citizen", a term it is often confused with, denotes a status shared by citizens of the United Kingdom, of British colonies and of independent States within the Commonwealth. For historical reasons, citizens of the Republic of Ireland, although not British subjects, are treated, in this and in other respects, as if they were.

If, as is more likely, the shipowner is a company, that company will be regarded as British if it is established under the laws of a Commonwealth country and has its principal place of business there. The first requirement is not difficult to apply. It is easy to discover where a company is registered. The second is more difficult and involves an examination of the internal company organisation. The nationality and residence of the shareholders and the directors of the company is an important factor, but may not be crucial. In *The Polzeath* [1916] P. 241, a company whose majority shareholder and effective director was a British subject and who did business in Germany and England was held, nonetheless, to have a principal place of business in Germany. It is conceivable, therefore, that a ship owned by a company registered under the British Company Acts, wholly owned by British shareholders, whose board was dominated by British directors, might not yet be a British ship because the company transacted its business primarily, say, in Uruguay. However, if it was intended to acquire a Uruguayan character for the ship, it would be more certain if the company were established and registered according to Uruguayan law.

To sum up, if a shipowner whose national character is British, according to the rules just discussed, owns a ship that ship should be registered as British under the Merchant Shipping Act. Of course, the rules of other countries may not be quite so strict as the British—although some are considerably stricter—and it may be possible, *as a matter of the law of that country*, for the British shipowner to register his ship there. However, the Merchant Shipping Acts still apply and, should the vessel ever come within the jurisdiction of a Court which applies those Acts, there will be a breach of the Act and the shipowner may suffer the penalties provided by the Acts: detention of his vessel and a fine.

3. British-controlled foreign ships

British persons and companies may and often do have interests in foreign registered vessels. Clearly, if British capital is invested in a foreign ship which is owned by a company established and doing business in a foreign country, no legal problems ensue. The owning company, although financially it may be predominantly British, has not the character of "Britishness" within the terms of the Merchant Shipping Acts and is therefore not subject to the relevant provisions.

A ship which is British within the definition in the Act which is not registered as a British ship is placed in the worst of all possible worlds. It may take no benefits under the Merchant Shipping Acts, but it remains liable to all the penalties, punishments or forfeitures which would apply if it were registered as a British ship (Merchant Shipping Act 1894, section 72).

4. Foreign ships

A ship improperly registered as a British ship (that is, one whose owner has not the necessary quality of "Britishness") may be forefeited by virtue of section 51(2) of the Merchant Shipping Act 1906. In this context it must, however, be remembered that it is not difficult for a foreign shipowner wishing to register his vessel as a British ship to acquire the necessary quality. A company, registered under the British Companies Acts, operating in this country will make a perfectly British shipowner, wherever the investment comes from. In addition, individuals who are citizens of any Commonwealth country, or of the Republic of Ireland, count as British subjects for this purpose.

5. The mechanics of registration

Registration is carried out by Registrars at Ports of Registry. Ports of registry are approved as such, in the United Kingdom, by the Commissioners of Customs and Excise. There are different procedures used for establishing registrars and ports of registry outside the United Kingdom.

Registrars are responsible to the Registrar-General of Shipping and Seamen, who is an official, with a department, within the Board of Trade, appointed by and responsible to the Secretary of State for Trade and Industry. Registrars must make monthly returns of new registries and other "current action" on their registers and a twice-yearly general return of vessels on their register. However, the day-to-day operation of registration is the responsibility of the registrar in the port of registry.

Before a vessel can be registered, it must be surveyed. This is done by a Surveyor of Ships, an official appointed as such by the Secretary of State. The purpose of a pre-registration survey is to establish an accurate description of the ship for the register. The survey, therefore, fixes the vessel's registered tonnage. Tonnage is a conventional measurement of the ship's size, and is based upon its cubic capacity, with certain allowed deductions so as to give it some commercial measure. The rules of measurement are set out in regulations, based upon international agreement. The surveyor also establishes the build of the ship and includes in his survey report any other facts as may be required from him by the Secretary of State from time to time. The report is made to the Secretary of State as well as for use in the process of registration.

Application for registration is made by the ship's owner. If the owner is, as is likely, a company, then the application must be made by a duly authorised agent of the company. The applicant must make a declaration of ownership and must state when and where the ship was built and the name of the ship's current master. He must also declare how many shares the ownership is divided into (as we have seen, a ship may be notionally divided into 64 shares for the purposes of ownership). If there is more than one owner, then the applicant must supply a list and must also declare that, to the best of his knowledge and belief, all others who are legally or beneficially entitled to any part of the ship are qualified to be owners of a registered British ship. That is, that they are British.

Ships must have names. The proposed name of the ship to be registered must be approved by the Registrar-General. A ship's name will not be accepted if it is already borne by an existing British registered ship, or if it is so close to one already on the register that it can be said to be "calculated to deceive". The name, once accepted, is part of the ship's registration and any alteration constitutes an alteration of the registry. The ship's name must be marked "permanently and conspicuously" in accordance with Board of Trade standards on both sides of her bow and on her stern and her Port of Registry must also appear on her stern. Further required markings include her registered tonnage and registration number, cut into her main beam, and a scale denoting her draught on both sides of her stem and on her stern-post. Required markings may not be altered, concealed or defaced.

Formalities over, the registrar will register the ship and enter her name in his Registry Book. The registry book of a port of registry is a permanent public record, accessible to those who might wish to examine it. Since the registration may also contain information as to mortgages (the use of the vessel as security), it must be clear that there may be good commercial reasons for examining a registry book. In addition, as we have noted, each registrar makes regular returns to the Registrar-General of Shipping and Seamen of the contents of his registry book.

Registration clearly indicates ownership. This fact gives significance to the Certificate of Registry, a document issued by the registrar upon registration of a ship. The certificate is a running document of title to the ship. The intention is that it should not be separated from the ship. As we have seen, any British ship can be detained, in British waters, until such time as her certificate of registry be produced. The document may not be sold or used as security in any way which would prevent it being used in connection with the use and navigation of the ship.

6. Alteration and termination of registration

Any alterations of the register must be carried out by application to the registrar in the port of registry. The registry book, and the certificate of registry, cannot be lawfully altered in any other way. Alterations are likely to take one of two forms. The vessel may be physically altered in some way or its name or its port of registry may be changed. Such changes can be regarded as external changes. Secondly, there may be substantive changes to ownership or entitlement to the ship: sales, alterations in the list of owners in multiple-owned ships, mortgages, or other security transactions, which give a lender a contingent entitlement.

The procedure required does not differ in accordance with whether the alteration is external or substantial. However, substantial changes affect other legal questions and will be considered again later. For the present, the point to be made is that none of these transactions, external or substantive, will be legally complete and effective until a formal alteration of the registry book, and of the certificate of registry, is effected, by application to the registrar in the ship's port of registry.

British-registered ships will leave the British register in a variety of circumstances. They may cease to exist. They may be totally lost, for example, by fire or perils of the sea, or they may be constructively totally lost, that is, so damaged that the cost of repair and recovery exceeds their salved value. A ship may be broken up. It may be captured by the enemy in time of war. In all these circumstances, the registered owner ought to surrender the certificate of registry (assuming it is still within his power to do so) and apply for the registration to be cancelled.

Alternatively, a British-registered ship may cease to be registrable as a British ship. Commonly, it may be sold to a non-British owner. More complexly, the character of the owner may change: for example, the owning company might cease to be regarded as British because its principal place of business might be changed from the United Kingdom to some other country. In these cases, too, the British certificate should be surrendered and the registration cancelled. A ship that *was* British but is no longer runs the risk of forfeiture as an improperly registered vessel.

7. Owners, managing owners and the ship's husband

The owner of a ship, like the owner of any property, has the legal right to use and exploit his property, within the general limits of the law, as he or she pleases. A shipowning company commonly exploits the vessel by way of charter-party, contracts which, to a greater or lesser extent, devolve the control of the vessel to others, for a consideration. Specifically, if the ship is chartered by demise, the shipowner will give up his right of possession and control to the charterer, who, for many purposes, will stand in the shoes of the owner.

That particular situation apart, however, the shipowner is the person primarily responsible for the ship and primarily entitled to use and exploit it. The master of the ship is generally the servant of the owners and will be treated as agent of the owner when, for example, he signs a bill of lading, unless the other contracting party has notice of a different circumstance. Again, the owner is in principle liable for the wages of the crew. The owner is the person responsible under the great majority of the public obligations imposed on shipping by the Merchant Shipping Acts.

Practical problems arise with multiple ownership. It is clear that part-owners are all liable in respect of the "ship's liabilities". They are partners in a commercial adventure. There are legal provisions which on the one hand seek to ensure that a majority of part-owners (called "the majority owners") shall have the ultimate authority over a ship and, on the other, that the minority can voice their objections to the running of the ship. The Court has jurisdiction to hear applications from majority and from minority and a wide power to restrain dealings with the ship.

It is, of course, wise for multiple owners of a ship to appoint one of their number as managing owner. A managing owner has the authority to deal with and exploit the ship on behalf of the other owners, and they are bound by his authorised actions. The name of a managing owner must be registered at the port of registry as such.

It may be that the shipowners—or the single shipowner—would wish to obtain the benefits of appointing a managing agent to operate the vessel who is not an owner. Such a manager would have similar powers and authority to the managing owner but, not being an owner, is called instead the "ship's husband". A ship's husband must also be registered as such.

For some purposes, managing owners and ship's husbands are treated as owners. For example, they are placed under a duty to report a shipping casualty affecting "their" ship (Merchant Shipping Act 1970, section 73(1)).

In modern times, the management of ships is commonly carried on, professionally, by managing companies which are not the actual owners of the ships in question. The powers and authority of such managers depends, of course, only upon the terms of the agreement made between them and the owners. Strictly, such companies are ship's husbands and, as managers of ships, should be registered as such.

8. Transfer, transmission and mortgage of ships

Ships, like other pieces of property, may be manufactured, dealt in and used as security for loans. They might even be inherited. The terms upon which these transactions are made and carried out are, of course, substantially a matter for the parties to the transaction in question, who will make their contracts subject to whatever terms please them. These terms, within the overall limits imposed by the law, will, if necessary, be legally enforced in the Courts.

Shipbuilding, ship-selling, ship-financing are all areas of skilled commercial activity and, as might be expected, standard forms of contracting have been developed in many areas over the years. For our present purposes it is necessary only to point out that such contracts exist and are used.

The law also imposes certain formalities, however. A transfer of a British-registered ship to a British transferee involves a necessary amendment to the registry book in the ship's port of registry. That amendment cannot be carried out without the presentation of two documents. The first is a Bill of Sale. A bill of sale is a formal written contract of sale. Apart from in connection with ships, bills of sale are scarcely ever used in an absolute form, though they do occur as conditional bills, designed to secure loans on goods. A ship's bill of sale is *not* conditional. It is a recital that the ship is sold to the purchaser. In form, by the Merchant Shipping Act 1894, the bill must correspond "as nearly as possible" to that set out in the first Schedule to the Merchant Shipping Act 1894 (Form A). A ship, then, is almost the only example of an article in commerce for which the law requires formality for its effective disposition.

Accompanying the executed Bill of Sale there must be a declaration signed by the transferee to the effect that he is qualified to be the owner of the ship. This, in effect, is a declaration that he has the necessary attribute of being British. For an individual, this means that he must be a British subject or a citizen of the Republic of Ireland; for a company, that it is incorporated by the laws of a country within the British Commonwealth and that it has its principal place of business there.

If a British-registered ship is to be transferred to a person not qualified to be the owner, the only formality required is notice to the appropriate registrar, who will take the ship off the British register. If the vessel never was British registered, there are, of course, no formalities at all.

If the transaction takes place outside the country in which the ship's port of registry is situated, then the procedure is replaced by another whereby the transferor submits the necessary information to the registrar who will then issue a Certificate of Sale. Similar provisions apply to mortgages executed outside the relevant country.

If a British-registered ship is acquired by *transmission*, that is, by inheritance, bankruptcy or any other way whereby property is transferred not by specific voluntary transaction but by operation of law, the person receiving the ship must make a declaration of transmission to the registrar, who will then make appropriate alteration to the register.

A mortgage is a transaction whereby a shipowner borrows money and uses the ship as security for the loan. Thus, the lender, the mortgagee, is given the right to look for his money in the value of the ship, if he is not repaid. A form (Form B) is provided by the Merchant Shipping Act 1894 for mortgages. A mortgage, in form which corresponds "as nearly as possible" to Form B, will be recorded by the registrar on presentation to him. There is no requirement that a mortgage be registered thus. Unregistered mortgages are still good contracts. However, if there is more than one mortgage, a registered mortgage takes priority over an unregistered mortgage, and will be paid first. Registered mortgages take priority among themselves according to their date of registration (not the date on which they are made). It is obviously in the interest of the mortgagee to see to it that his mortgage is registered as quickly as possible. Unregistered mortgages, also called "equitable mortgages," rank in accordance with their dates of execution.

A mortgagee's rights over the ship are essentially contingent. So long as he is being paid in accordance with his contract he has no need to interfere with the operation of the vessel. However, should he need to involve himself, he has power to enter into possession, to run the ship and take the profits and to dispose of it. At no time, of course, is he entitled to keep more than what is owing to him.

The system of registration as it applies to transactions such as these which we have been describing is generally supervised by the Courts, which have a general power to prohibit dealing in a ship on the application of a party interested. In this way entitlements can be tested.

CHAPTER 14

INTRODUCTION TO MARITIME ARBITRATION

The referring of disputes to arbitration enables the parties to put their case in private before a tribunal of their own choosing, usually composed of arbitrators who are themselves knowledgeable about the subject matter of the dispute and, if it be the wish of the parties, sometimes with the added bonus of speed and economy.

However, it is inevitable in modern society that there will be some measure of judicial review of the arbitral process, and to understand this review it is necessary to look at Arbitration Acts which apply today. Although it is not possible to cover it in this chapter, students would do well to study the history of arbitration and the merits of the competing arguments of finality and legality.

Since the 1979 Act became law and took effect on arbitrations commenced on and after Aug. 1, 1979, innumerable articles have been written about it, seminars have been devoted to it, and talks have been delivered by lawyers and arbitrators in almost every commercial centre around the world. In spite of all this dissemination of information, other than the lawyers specialising in arbitration, and practising arbitrators themselves, together with a few keen "customers" of arbitration, there is still much ignorance amongst commercial men about the Act, as indeed there always was about the 1950 Act.

One of the reasons for this ignorance must be that, when negotiating a contract, usually the last thing a broker or a principal is thinking about is a dispute, and scant consideration is given to the wording of the arbitration clause itself, other than perhaps sometimes to consider the venue. This leads even today, in cases where a printed arbitration clause is not included in the contract, to the importation of woolly and unsatisfactory clauses such as "Arbitration London" or "Arbitration London in the customary manner", which can lead to unimagined complications.

Part of the job of a broker when negotiating a contract is to find out what his principal requires of various clauses, but how often does a broker ask his principal if, as far as the arbitration clause is concerned, he wishes the clause to provide for a sole arbitrator to be agreed between the parties, or for an arbitrator to be appointed by each side with, in the event of disagreement, power to the said two arbitrators to appoint an umpire, or for a tribunal of three arbitrators with, if necessary, a majority decision prevailing?

Suitable clauses covering the above alternatives would be:—

"Any dispute arising under the Charterparty shall be referred to a Sole Arbitrator in London agreed by the parties. If the parties fail to agree upon a Sole Arbitrator, then each party to appoint an arbitrator and, in case the arbitrators shall not agree, then to the decision of an Umpire to be appointed by them. The Award of the Arbitrator(s) or the Umpire shall be final and binding upon both parties".

"Any dispute arising under the Charterparty shall be referred to three persons in London, one to be appointed by each of the parties hereto and the third by the two so chosen; their decision, or that of any two of them, shall be final".

In addition, there are many sophisticated clauses available to choose from which cater for the requirements of parties to almost any contract. If a broker is uncertain of how to word an arbitration clause, or if he needs guidance on arbitration procedure, he will almost certainly receive a sympathetic hearing and advice from any of the practising arbitrators.

In order to understand the 1979 Act it is necessary to have an understanding of the two other Acts that remain on the Statute Book, the 1950 Act (known as the Principal Act), and the 1975 Act. The Arbitration Act 1950 consolidated prior legislation on arbitration, of which the Arbitration Act 1889 was the principal statute. The Arbitration Act 1975 gave effect to the 1958 New York Convention on the Recognition and Enforcement of Arbitral Awards. The Arbitration Act 1979 amended English law on arbitration, amongst other things abolishing the "Case Stated" procedure, replacing it with a limited form of judicial review, and made other changes, the most important of which will be discussed in this chapter. Every broker should have copies of the three Acts readily available, and should make a study of them.

Efficient and popular as it was, the English arbitration system prior to the 1979 Act had defects, and for some years dissatisfaction had been expressed with some aspects of the 1950 Act, particularly the Case Stated system, which allowed or, if the Court so ordered, compelled an arbitrator to state his award in the form of a Special Case, i.e. to find the facts and to submit any questions of law arising for decision by the High Court. This system was sometimes misused by respondents solely for the purpose of delay. If the arbitrator refused to state his award in the form of a Special Case because, for example, no question of law arose on the facts as he saw them, the respondent could apply to the Court. At this stage no award had been made and the Court, not knowing why the arbitrator had refused the application, would usually order him to make his award in this form. Once this had been done, either party had an unfettered right of appeal not only to the High Court, but also to the Court of Appeal and, with leave, to the House of Lords.

Objections to the Case Stated procedure were based not only on the delay occasioned by the judicial review, but also on the fact that the arbitral process was subject to judicial intervention at all. This latter objection became more formidable with the increase of supranational contracts, usually in engineering and construction contracts for projects in developing countries, often involving governments or government agencies who were unprepared for their disputes to be reviewed by the Courts of another country.

In 1977 the Lord Chancellor set up the Commercial Court Committee to provide a direct link between the commercial users of the Commercial Court and the Court itself, and thereby to improve the service which the Court was able to offer. The Committee's terms of reference were to consider and keep under review the working of the Commercial Court and the arbitration Special Case procedure and to make such recommendations to the Lord Chancellor as may seem from time to time to be necessary.

In July, 1979, the Commercial Court Committee issued a report recommending changes in the law governing arbitration. The Government accepted the majority of the Committee's recommendations and a Bill was presented to Parliament which eventually became the Arbitration Act 1979.

The 1979 Act is broadly designed to make London arbitration more effective and more attractive, and it sets out to do this in more or less nine different ways:—

1. It removes from the Court its power to remit or set aside an award for an error of fact or law on its face. This power was the cause of arbitrators making awards without reasons ("non-speaking" or "non-motivated") or, when giving reasons, putting these reasons in a separate document under reserves. No arbitrator should now fear giving a reasoned award ("speaking" or "motivated").

2. It repeals section 21 of the Principal Act—the provision relating to the Special Case. For several years there will still be awards made in the form of Special Cases where the arbitrations were commenced before Aug. 1, 1979, although it is open to the parties in these arbitrations to agree that the 1979 Act shall apply.

3. It provides for a new appeal procedure. As this is one of the most important provisions of the new Act, it is quoted in full, as follows:—

> Section 1(2)
>
> Subject to subsection (3) below, an appeal shall lie to the High Court on any question of law arising out of an award made on an arbitration agreement; and on the determination of such an appeal the High Court may by order—
>
> (a) confirm, vary or set aside the award; or
>
> (b) remit the award to the reconsideration of the arbitrator or umpire together with the court's opinion on the question of law which was the subject of the appeal;

and where the award is remitted under paragraph (b) above the arbitrator or umpire shall, unless the order otherwise directs, make his award within three months after the date of the order.

The automatic right to appeal from the High Court to the Court of Appeal is removed. The Act makes it necessary to obtain the leave of the High Court or the Court of Appeal and, in addition, the High Court has to certify that the question of law to which its decision relates either is one of general public importance or is one which for some other special reason should be considered by the Court of Appeal.

4. It provides for the prevention of abuse of the appeal procedure. This provision of the Court's powers to impose terms will probably be the most important provision in practice of avoiding delay. The High Court will not grant leave to appeal automatically just because some question of law is involved in the reference. It will have to be satisfied that the resolution of this question of law could substantially affect the rights of the parties. Furthermore, in granting leave to appeal the High Court can impose conditions, such as that the sum awarded be secured or paid into Court.

Application for leave to appeal must be made within 21 days of the award being made and published to the parties or, if an order is made by the Court requiring the arbitrator to give reasons or further reasons, within 21 days from the date on which the reasons are given. Many consider that 21 days is too short a period and that 42 days would be a better period.

5. It provides for reasoned awards. No arbitrator is obliged to give any reasons for his award, unless ordered to do so by the High Court, and the Court will not normally do so unless, before the award was made, one of the parties asked the arbitrator for a reasoned award. Nevertheless, it is anticipated that arbitrators will invariably give reasoned awards when asked to do so by one of the parties. This provision does not mean that virtually all awards will be reasoned, as they are not likely to be so in the "quality" type of arbitrations, and in some specialist fields, such as in the construction industry, where there are likely to be few such requests from the parties.

6. It provides for the hearing of preliminary issues of law arising in the course of the arbitration. The High Court is given power to determine preliminary points of law on application by any of the parties to the reference, provided the arbitrator consents or all the other parties consent. With this provision the Court must be satisfied that the question of law is one in respect of which leave to appeal against an award would be likely to be given, so it incorporates the requirement of section 1 that the determination of the disputed point could affect the rights of one or more of the parties substantially. In addition it requires that the Court is satisfied that the determination of a preliminary point may produce substantial savings in costs to the parties.

7. It provides for an Exclusion Agreement. This is another most important provision, and one that has perhaps caused more controversy than almost any other part of the Act. The new procedure enables the parties to exclude altogether the right of appeal from the award, which would lead to the exclusion of the power of the Court to require the arbitrator to give reasons, and the right to request judicial determination of a preliminary point of law, although it does not preclude the jurisdiction of the Court to correct "misconduct" on the part of arbitrators.

The parties to any contract may enter into a valid exclusion agreement provided it is entered into after the commencement of the arbitration concerned, or where the proper law of the contract is other than English law.

Other than as mentioned above, parties to domestic arbitration agreements may not enter into valid exclusion agreements, and the same applies to international arbitrations in Special Category Disputes. Special Category Disputes are defined as disputes falling within the Admiralty jurisdiction of the High Court, disputes arising out of insurance contracts, and disputes arising out of commodity contracts. Maritime disputes fall within the Admiralty jurisdiction of the High Court.

The Special Category Dispute Section was designed to preserve the link between the Courts and those categories of international arbitration which make the principal contribution to the development of English Commercial Law, namely, shipping, insurance and the commodity trading contracts.

The Act, however, provides for the Secretary of State to restrict the category of the Special Category Disputes hereafter, so it is possible that these restrictions on the making of a valid exclusion agreement might be relaxed in the future if there was evidence that the continued development of English Commercial Law would not be prejudiced by such a relaxation.

It will be seen that a valid exclusion agreement may be made at any time by parties to arbitrations arising out of international contracts for major construction, development and investment projects, as the Act would have eliminated the reservations that inhibited the use of London arbitration facilities and the adoption of English law by such parties in the past.

8. It provides for the making of Interlocutory Orders. Before the 1979 Act there was provision for an arbitrator to make a variety of interlocutory orders, but he had no effective means of enforcing them. He could apply to the High Court for certain useful orders, but even the High Court's powers were limited, and this gap in an arbitrator's powers afforded an opportunity for delaying tactics if one of the parties was so inclined. Section 5 of the 1979 Act provides that the High Court may empower the arbitrator to issue interlocutory orders penalising parties who fail to comply with the arbitrator's timetable or directions.

This new provision does not derogate any power the arbitrator previously had, and he may still proceed to an *ex parte* award under section 7(b). Now, upon an application by the arbitrator or any party to the reference, the Court may authorise the arbitrator to continue with the reference in the same manner as a judge could continue with ordinary Court proceedings.

9. It provides for minor amendments. Under the Principal Act, any agreement to refer disputes to three arbitrators (as in the arbitration clause of the New York Produce Exchange charter-party) took effect as an agreement to appoint two arbitrators and an umpire if the third arbitrator was to be appointed by the other two arbitrators, each of whom was appointed by one of the parties. This sometimes frustrated the intentions of the parties. One of the amendments enables effect to be given to the expressed intentions of the parties.

Also under the Principal Act, if a dispute was referred to two arbitrators they were required immediately to appoint an umpire. This caused needless expense if it was apparent to the arbitrators that they were likely to agree on the award, although maritime arbitrators, where they were in agreement and an umpire was unnecessary, tended to ignore this provision in the interest of economy of costs. The 1979 Act permits the two arbitrators to appoint an umpire at any time, but requires them to do so forthwith if they cannot agree.

Many disputants had become so used to the 1950 Act arbitrarily imposing on them, where appropriate, a tribunal including an umpire that they are now sometimes surprised that they are faced with a tribunal of three arbitrators, even when the arbitration clause calls for it! It should again be stressed that brokers should find out what the true intentions of the parties are in this respect and word the arbitration clause accordingly.

The Arbitration Act 1979 represents a compromise between the views of those in England who prize finality in arbitration awards above all, and those who insist on a rigid adherence to the principle of legality. The principle of English law that arbitrations must be conducted in accordance with settled principles of law has not been abandoned. However, substantial concessions in favour of the principle of finality have been made. Moreover, the Courts have been clothed with powers by state, and have developed new powers, which will enable them to act more effectively in support of arbitrations.

It is not claimed that the new system is perfect. On the contrary, the manner in which the 1979 Act is working is under review by the Commercial Court Committee with a view to recommendations for further reform. In fact a small sub-committee of the Commercial Court Committee has been established under the chairmanship of a High Court judge to study the problem and to report with its recommendations. Meantime it can be said that a not unreasonable balance has been found between the competing principles of finality and legality.

Finally, it is recommended that students of shipbroking, and indeed qualified and experienced shipbrokers, should study articles on arbitration and maritime law which appear regularly in the *Shipbroker, Lloyd's Maritime and Commercial Law Quarterly* and, in important cases, where appeals to the High Court have been granted, to read the full judgments. Apart from short reports which appear in *Lloyd's List, The Times,* and *The Financial Times,* the law reports themselves are available in the libraries of the Institute of Chartered Shipbrokers and of the Baltic Exchange.

CHAPTER 15

THE SHIPOWNER AS EMPLOYER

1. Introduction

There have been special laws governing the employment of seafarers for many years. Some of these rules derive from the special circumstances of maritime employment. Before the advent of modern systems of communications, the ship was a completely isolated community, out of the reach of ordinary legal and other procedures for perhaps months at a time. It was also subject to identifiable and particular risks. These facts necessitated the granting to the master of the ship powers in excess of those one would expect to find in the exercise of managerial authority at an equivalent level ashore.

The same practical background helps to explain the particular slant of safety rules applicable to ships. Again, the law seeks to regulate the manning of a ship to an extent which would be unheard of in similar land-based enterprises.

Other parts of maritime labour law derive from particular social or political problems, generally occurring in the 18th and 19th centuries. The careful regulation of the recruitment of seamen through "signing-on" ceremonies and ship's articles, seamen's allotments, repatriation rules and many others can be so traced.

Modern lawmakers have been faced with two problems. One is how far such law, apparently antique, should be changed in the light of modern conditions. The other is to what extent the new developments in general labour law, unfair dismissal, redundancy payments, legal protection of trade union activity, should be extended to the sea and with what qualifications, if any.

All this makes maritime employment law into an extremely complicated branch of labour law. What follows is a description of the peculiarities of maritime employment in that context. It is not, therefore, a comprehensive account of all the applicable law.

2. The seafarer's contract of employment

Every employee works under a contract of employment, which is the primary source of his legal rights and obligations. The Merchant Navy Established Service Scheme adds a complexity to the question of identifying that contract in maritime employment. Under the scheme, seafarers are registered and, unless they have a Company Service Contract, are allocated in accordance with the scheme to ships. Their registration with the Merchant Navy Establishment Authority is clearly a contract and they also have a contract of employment with each shipping company they work for. The two contracts are so intertwined, however, that for the purpose of discovering the binding terms applicable to the seafarer, they can be read together. A Company Service Contract is easier. It is a renewable fixed-term contract of employment between the seafarer and the shipping company and it persists beyond each voyage undertaken by the individual.

The terms of the contract of employment are strictly a matter for agreement in each case, but in practice the great bulk of the terms are to be discovered in collective agreements. The formalised structure of collective bargaining within the industry is the National Maritime Board. The decisions of the N.M.B. are generally regarded as incorporated into the terms of a seafarer's contract.

3. Crew agreements and crew lists

In order to protect seamen from exploitation with regard to the terms of their employment, and partly to deal with other abuses surrounding the recruitment of sailors for ships, the process of engagement has long been subject to legal regulation. Until the coming into force of the Merchant Shipping Act 1970, the process was called the signing of the ship's articles. The terms of the seamen's engagement were in written form, they were read to the (in earlier times usually illiterate) seafarer, then signed by the ship's master, on behalf of the owners, and the crew-member. All this under the supervision of an official of the Board of Trade called a Marine Superintendent. The 1970 Act seeks to simplify the procedure somewhat. The ship's articles are now called the "crew agreement" and the signing-on ceremony witnessed by the superintendent has been abolished.

By the Merchant Shipping (Crew Agreements, Lists of Crew and Discharge of Seamen) Regulations 1972, made under the Merchant Shipping Act 1970, section 1, the superintendent must be informed at least 24 hours before any seamen are signed on, unless no more than two seamen are involved or such notice would unreasonably delay the ship. In the event, he must receive a copy of the crew agreement and another copy must be posted conspicuously on board the ship. Any seaman governed by the crew agreement may demand a copy of it and the master of the ship must be able to produce a copy on demand by a Customs officer.

Crew lists are what the term implies. It is a list of all those employed on board the vessel—for once the master is included. In addition to names, much other information is included: the date and place of birth, next of kin, numbers of discharge books and certificates of competency and the date of commencement and discharge of each seafarer under his current contract. Three copies are required. One for the owner, one for the superintendent and the third to be kept in the ship for production to a Customs officer or superintendent on demand.

4. Discharge and discharge books

The signing-off of seamen at one time was subject to the same sort of ceremonial protection as that given to signing-on. Again, the detail of the procedure has been streamlined. The superintendent must be given 48 hours notice of discharge, if possible, and the discharge must take place in the presence of the master or other duly authorised representative of the shipowner. A seafarer with a company service contract will not be discharged at the end of each voyage: his leaving of his ship does not affect his continued employment.

Discharges abroad, unless both the seaman and the ship's master agree or it is necessary in the interests of safety or good order and discipline, or for the purpose of getting urgent medical attention, may not occur without the consent of the local British consul or, in a Commonwealth country, the superintendent or his equivalent. There are provisions to deal with emergencies.

Discharges must be accompanied by appropriate entries in the ship's official log and in the seaman's discharge book. A seaman's discharge book is in some sense his document of identification as a seafarer. As well as his name and personal details, it contains his MNEA number, his certificates of competency (if any) and a record of his training and employment. Discharge books no longer contain a record of the satisfactory, or other, nature of his performance, although separate certificates as to the quality of his work may be issued by the master only if the seaman so requests.

In addition to his discharge book, a British seaman also holds an identity card. This is little more than a short reference document, containing name, description, date of birth, nationality, address, and his national insurance and discharge book number. This card must be produced on demand to a superintendent, a foreign consular officer or his employer or master.

5. Wages

Traditionally, a seaman was employed by the voyage and for the voyage. Wages came if and when the vessel successfully completed that voyage. As a result, special rules were developed to protect the seaman and his dependents.

First, a seaman's wages are protected from the intervention of creditors. They may not be "attached." However, in some way as a qualification to this, he may make "allotments". An allotment is made by written direction, signed by the seaman, in approved form, of part of his wages to named dependents. There are limits both as to the amount of the allotment and the possible beneficiaries. Once made, an allotment note entitles the person named in it to the sums declared in it.

On discharge (which, it will be remembered, in the case of a seaman with a company service contract does *not* necessarily occur at the end of every voyage), a seaman is entitled to a full statement of account of what is owed to him at least 24 hours beforehand. If more than £50 is owing to him, he is entitled to £50 or one quarter of the total, whichever is greater, immediately upon discharge, and the balance within seven days. Otherwise, he is entitled to the whole at once.

The superintendent has jurisdiction to hear and determine disputes about wages.

6. Repatriation

A seaman unfortunate enough to be shipwrecked and not to have a service contract which survives the disaster is statutorily entitled to a further two months' wages after his agreement has been terminated by the unexpected end to the voyage.

Shipwrecked seamen have another problem, whether or not their wages are protected. They are often stranded in a foreign country. The same is true of those who fall sick or suffer injuries or who are discharged abroad. The Merchant Shipping Acts, now sections 62-64 of the Merchant Shipping Act 1970, impose upon the last employer of such a seaman the obligation to maintain him until his repatriation and to bring him home. Expenses incurred by the British Government, or by a foreign government, or by the stranded seaman himself, may be claimed from that employer. However, a seaman's claim may be defeated if his being stranded was attributable to "his own wrongful act or neglect". The detailed rules and procedures are to be found in the Merchant Shipping (Repatriation) Regulations 1972.

7. Health, safety and welfare

Standards for health and welfare of seafarers are set by several different sets of regulations. The Merchant Shipping (Crew Accommodation) Regulations 1953, with their amendments govern heating, lighting, ventilation, soundproofing and water-supply as well as, in more general terms, the construction and placing of crew accommodation on board a ship. The power to make further regulations, which commonly come about as a result of the adoption of internationally agreed standards, is now contained in section 20 of the Merchant Shipping Act 1970. The adequacy of the supply of food and fresh water is governed by section 21 of the same Act and by the Merchant Shipping (Provisions and Water) Regulations 1972. There is a statutory right of complaint. If three or more seamen are dissatisfied with the quality or quantity of the food or water they may complain that it is not in accordance with the regulations. Such complaint goes, in the first instance, to the ship's master: if they are not satisfied, they may complain further to the superintendent or, if abroad, to the appropriate consular official or, in a Commonwealth country, to the superintendent or his equivalent.

Whether a ship's doctor is carried is a question to be answered by the manning rules (see later). At present, by the Merchant Shipping Act 1894, section 209, foreign-going ships carrying more than 100 persons must carry a doctor. Other ships may. If no doctor is carried, the master must designate a member of the crew to treat sick crew members (Merchant Shipping Act 1970, section 25). All ships must carry medical supplies in accordance with the Merchant Shipping (Medical Scales) Regulations 1974, as amended. If a seaman is in need of medical attention abroad, the cost must be borne by the employer—even to the extent of the cost of his funeral (Merchant Shipping Act 1970, section 26).

The traditional approach to maritime safety concentrated upon rendering the vessel safe as a ship: thus the law contains provisions as to load lines and life-saving equipment, all designed to meet specifically maritime perils. To this could be added ship construction rules and provisions for survey, which, together with the general requirement of seaworthiness, are intended to ensure that ships are safe conveyances. Manning and certification is also a matter of safety: skillful and competent officers should mean a safe voyage. However, until the Health and Safety at Work, etc. Act 1974 came into force, the general laws relating to safe workplaces was not applied to ships.

The 1974 Act does apply to ships. The word "premises" which is highly significant for the application of the Act is, by section 53, expressly defined so as to include any ship or vessel. Further, although in general Acts of Parliament apply only within the territorial limits of the country, there is express power to extend the Health and Safety at Work Act to the high seas or other places outside territorial waters (section 84). This power has been used in respect of offshore oil installations and attendant structures and there is no doubt that it could be used to apply to ships. In any case, the Act as it stands applies to ships, of whatever registration, when in British territorial waters.

As yet, the Act is essentially a structure for the future development of the law. It created a system of public authorities, the Health and Safety Commission and the Health and Safety Executive, who, with the Secretary of State for Employment, are given the responsibility of enforcing the present occupational safety laws and, through the enactment of regulations and codes of practice, of updating and extending those laws. Currently, occupational safety statutes such as the Factories Act 1961, have little or no effect upon ships (except when they are in dry dock): the clear intention to apply the Health and Safety at Work Act to shipping, however, would indicate that in future the law will be applied to ships specifically.

The Health and Safety at Work Act, however, is not only an enabling Act for future action. Until the law is extended and developed, the "leeway" is to be made up by the "general duties". There are six of these and they are set out in the first part of the Act. In general, they are written in the language of "reasonable practicability". Thus, section 2 imposes on all employers the duty "to ensure, so far as is reasonably practicable, the health, safety and welfare at work of all his employees". Section 4 imposes duties in similar terms in respect of the safety of premises to those who are not in the employment of the "occupier" of those premises who use them for work. As we have seen, "premises" includes ships. The combined effect of sections 2 and 4 would, therefore, seem to be that, whoever employs the crew, both owner and charterer of a ship are likely to find themselves under some sort of legal duty imposed by the 1974 Act.

Not all the general duties are as general as those just described. Section 2(2), for example, fills out the wide employer's duty quoted above (which appears in section 2(1)) by requiring the provision of safe plant and "systems of work", a safe workplace, the safe storage and handling of "articles and substances" and a safe, healthy and salubrious "working environment". In each case, the duty is to effect this "so far as is reasonably practicable". Perhaps of greater practical significance, the same sub-section imposes a similar duty to provide "such information, instruction, training and supervision as is necessary to ensure, so far as is reasonably practicable, the health and safety at work" of the employees.

There is a general duty in section 7 which imposes upon employees the obligation to take reasonable care of themselves and others. Section 8 supplements this by imposing specific duties to co-operate with the employer in safety matters and not to misuse safety equipment.

From October, 1978, there has been a compulsory system of Safety Representatives and Safety Committees and a duty on the employer to consult with such persons. Statutory safety representatives, who are chosen by the trade union if one is recognised, have certain rights, including a right to inspect the premises for risks and the right to communicate with the Health and Safety Inspectorate.

Finally, the general duties of the employer include a duty to have and to publish a statement of the employer's safety policy, together with the administrative arrangements currently in force for carrying it out. The safety policy is a document which must be brought to the attention of the employees.

The general duties are enforced by the Health and Safety Executive, through its inspectors, in exactly the same way as any other part of occupational safety law. Breach is a criminal offence, for which offenders may be prosecuted and fined. In addition, the Health and Safety at Work Act has introduced two new methods of enforcement: the improvement notice and the prohibition notice.

An improvement notice is issued by an inspector to any "person" (including a company), and specifies that a breach of the Health and Safety at Work Act (or of any relevant regulation or other occupational safety statute) has occurred. It requires that it be remedied by a stated date. It may, but need not, specify *how* the breach should be remedied. The notice may be appealed against, either on its legality or its reasonableness, to an Industrial Tribunal. If no appeal is taken, or if one is taken but fails, then the notice must be complied with. It is an offence that it has not been complied with and the legality or reasonableness of the notice cannot be raised at this late stage.

A prohibition notice is similar in form to an improvement notice. However, a prohibition notice is based not upon a breach of any law but upon a risk of personal injury or injury to health. It does not, therefore, direct that some specific breach be remedied, it orders that the condition which gave rise to the risk should stop.

These procedures, based upon the general duties contained in the first part of the Act, can clearly be applied to ships.

In addition, the Merchant Shipping Act 1979 contains a section empowering the Secretary of State to issue safety regulations for ships. The power has not yet been exercised.

8. Manning and certification

There have been compulsory standards requiring ships to carry certain numbers of properly certificated officers for over 130 years. The result of the imposition of those standards was the development by the Board of Trade of examinations and testing for the award of Certificates of Competency. Board of Trade certificates, however, have in a sense for many years stood upon their own feet. They are a useful public declaration of maritime competence and are worth having on that ground alone. The Board of Trade, indeed, issues certificates which are not required by the "statutory scale" laid down in the Merchant Shipping Acts.

The Merchant Shipping Act 1970 contains provisions which will lead, eventually, to a major restructuring of the system of manning and certification, so as to provide a more comprehensive coverage and much greater flexibility. So far, these powers have been used only in respect of deck and engineering officers. The appropriate regulations were promulgated in 1977 and came into force in 1981. There are complex provisions relating to carry-over and equivalence.

Both old and new schemes primarily apply to officers. An exception is the requirement, in section 5 of the Merchant Shipping Act 1948, that every person employed as an able seaman on board a United Kingdom-registered ship must hold a certificate of competency as such or he may not be entered on the Crew List. Otherwise, the law specifies the numbers and appropriate levels of certificated competency of master, navigating officers, engineering officers and radio officers. There are also requirements as to cooks, lifeboatmen and medical officers. The levels are, in general, set by reference to the ship's size and her voyage—where she is going.

Enforcement of manning levels under the old law was essentially that contained in section 459 of the Merchant Shipping Act 1894, which made it an offence to send a dangerously unseaworthy ship to sea and, more important, allowed its detention until the unseaworthiness be remedied. Undermanning, or lack of duly certificated personnel, was clearly and expressly an aspect of unseaworthiness. The statutory obligations, as set out in the "statutory scale" could, for the purpose of the powers under section 459, be supplemented less formally. This was done by official "notices to mariners" which set out desirable deck-manning, for instance.

The enforcement of the new law is contained in section 45 of the Merchant Shipping Act 1970 which makes it a specific offence for a ship to go to sea, or attempt to do so, while undermanned in terms of the new law. The offence is committed by the "owner or the master" and that phrase, used in other contexts in maritime law, seems to mean that *both* the owner *and* the master may be successfully prosecuted for an offence under the section. (See *The Huntingdon* [1974] 1 Lloyd's Rep. 520).

Under both old and new law it is an offence to serve as a qualified officer or seaman if one is not so qualified.

9. Discipline

One of the most distinctive peculiarities of maritime employment law is that there have always been wide disciplinary powers granted to the master of the ship. These powers are not only more extensive than those available to a shore-based manager with equivalent responsibilities, they are supported by specific civil and criminal consequences.

The disciplinary authority of the master is very ancient. It exists as a common law power and can be traced back for several hundred years. In a broad sense, the master may put crew-members under restraint and punish them if he acts in order to preserve the safety of the ship or to preserve good order and discipline. However, his actions must be genuinely directed to that end if they are to be justified. In *Hook* v. *Cunard* [1953] 1 All E.R. 1051, the master of the *Queen Elizabeth* imprisoned a steward on the complaint of a passenger, whose young daughter had, somewhat doubtfully, identified him as responsible for an indecent assault she alleged to have occurred. In a general sense, such action would seem eminently justifiable: however, the steward was released within an hour of the disembarkation of the first-class passengers at New

York, which indicated that the master had believed the steward's story rather than that of the complainant. The imprisonment was, therefore, not carried out in order to preserve order and discipline, but to satisfy an angry and emotional passenger.

This common law power is exercisable also over passengers (see *King* v. *Franklin* (1858) 1 F. & F. 361)—indeed it is said that Sir Walter Raleigh once hanged a passenger for disobeying his orders. He was, however, the master of a privateer.

These wide powers began to be brought under statutory controls in the 1850s. Currently, the master's powers of arrest and restraint are to be found in section 79 of the Merchant Shipping Act 1970. This entitles him to "cause any person on board to be put under restraint if and for so long as it appears to him to be necessary and expedient in the interest of safety or for the preservation of good order or discipline aboard the ship". The section is clearly not limited to action taken against crew members: it can apply to "any person". By section 77 stowing away is made an offence and by section 78 it is an offence to go on board or remain in the ship without the consent of the master. (This last provision owes its origin to legislation against "crimps", usually lodging-house keepers, who acted as seamen's employment agents and regularly intercepted their wages.)

The Merchant Shipping Act 1894, sections 287 and 288, gives the master power to arrest passengers for a variety of offences, including drunkenness, failure to pay a fare, molesting or obstructing the crew and molesting a passenger. When arrested, such persons are to be conveyed to a Justice of the Peace for formal charging.

Crew members are made subject to specific criminal and civil liabilities. Over recent years, this has been an area of considerable debate: the law has been substantially changed by three statutes, The Merchant Shipping Acts 1970, 1974 and 1979. Although the final amendments are not yet in force, the pattern has clearly emerged. The scheme is in three parts. At the top of the list comes the special application of the criminal law—criminal offences committed by seafarers who behave badly at sea. Second comes disciplinary offences, the clearest application of the master's authority over the crew: it is here that the greatest dissatisfaction has been expressed. The right of an employer to fine employees is for all practical purposes unknown away from the sea and this right is substantially attacked by the 1979 Act. Finally, there are some civil consequences of maritime industrial misbehaviour—especially obligations to pay for the consequences of misconduct.

There are now three criminal offences which may be committed by an undisciplined seaman. These are set out in the Merchant Shipping Act 1970. They are the offence of endangering the ship (section 27), the offence of drunkenness (section 28) and persistent or concerted disobedience or neglect of duty (section 30). Until the passage of the Merchant Shipping Act 1974 a single act of disobedience by one person was an offence, provided the disobedience was wilful, but that was repealed by section 19 of the 1974 Act. Now disobedience to lawful commands is only a crime if persistent or concerted—that is, if it continues over a period of time or is the result of agreement between several seamen. This last point clearly affects industrial action, which is described below. Section 19 of the 1974 Act also abolished the offence of being absent without leave at the time of sailing: this matter is now dealt with in terms of the civil law.

As we have said, the present law on disciplinary offences is under sentence of death. The sentence has not yet been formally carried out, however, so some notice should be taken of the system described by the Merchant Shipping Act 1970, sections 34-38, and the Merchant Shipping (Disciplinary Offences) Regulations 1972, as amended in 1974. Those regulations set out a variety of disciplinary offences, including wilful disobedience to a lawful command, wilfully striking another person, drunkenness, being asleep on duty, failing to be available for duty, being in possession of an offensive weapon, being in possession of the property of another, damaging the ship, smuggling unauthorised persons on board, smoking in a prohibited area, etc. Disciplinary offences were dealt with by the master. The punishment was a fine. Fines could be remitted for subsequent good behaviour and if not were deducted from wages on discharge and paid to the superintendent. Appeals lay to the superintendent.

One suggested modification of the master's "autocratic" authority was the creation of ship's disciplinary committees to exercise his authority. Provisions for creating such bodies were contained in section 35 of the 1970 Act but that section was never brought into effect.

The current replacement for the master's authority is to refer the matter, as a complaint by the master, to a shore-based body with the power to reprimand and, in effect, to confiscate the offender's discharge book, thus affecting his chances of obtaining further employment. This system is intended to operate within agreed Codes of Practice. A code was agreed between the trade unions and the General Council of British Shipping and came into force in 1979. Section 23 of the Merchant Shipping Act 1979 gives the Secretary of State power to make regulations to give legal effect to such a code and, at the same time, repeals the relevant sections of the 1970 Act. However, section 23 of the 1979 Act has not yet been brought into force. Thus the code of practice operates by agreement. The law has not yet been changed.

The scheme of civil liability is designed to deal with seamen who are absent without leave. Such persons are, of course, in breach of their contracts of employment, like any other employee in similar circumstances. It is not, however, common for employees to be sued for breaking their contracts of employment. In the case of seamen, the right to sue is specially controlled by the Merchant Shipping Acts.

The seaman is given the special defence that his absence was "due to an accident or mistake or some other cause beyond his control". This would not, in the general law, be a good defence to a breach of contract action. Secondly, his liability is limited to £10 if no loss has been shown to be attributable to his absence and £100 if loss did result. In addition, if the shipowner because of a seaman's absence in a foreign country is fined for breaking the immigration laws, that fine can be recovered from the seaman. There are similar provisions with regard to seamen who break the law by smuggling.

10. Industrial action and trade unions

The law of industrial disputes is in general much the same at sea as on land. Some of the differences have been removed by section 43 of the Merchant Shipping Act 1970 and by the general application to all forms of employment, maritime and non-maritime, of the Trade Union and Labour Relations Act 1974 and the Employment Protection (Consolidation) Act 1978. It is not necessary here to describe the whole law of industrial action and trade unions.

However, there was one particular legal problem involved in the consideration of maritime industrial action. Since it remains a criminal offence for seamen to "combine to disobey lawful commands, to neglect duty or to impede the progress of the ship" seriously intended industrial action by seamen *at sea* would seem likely to be criminal. This difficulty was met by section 42(2) of the 1970 Act which gives a statutory right to a seaman "to terminate his employment in that ship by leaving the ship in contemplation or furtherance of a trade dispute after giving to the master not less than 48 hours' notice of his intention to do so and shall not be compelled . . . to go to sea in the 48 hours following the giving of such a notice; but such notice shall be of no effect unless at the time it was given the ship is in the United Kingdom and securely moored in a safe berth".

Several points should be noted. "In contemplation or furtherance of a trade dispute" has a precise and often complicated meaning in general labour law. It applies to genuine disputes about wages, conditions of work, etc., and does not apply to "political" strikes. Second, the right to give 48 hours notice only applies to a proper strike—the ceasing of work. "Working to rule" and other lesser pieces of industrial action are not covered by the section. The striking seamen must leave the ship. Finally and obviously the right applies only to home-port based strikes. It has no effect abroad or at sea.

Under the Trade Union and Labour Relations Act 1974 and the Employment Protection (Consolidation) Act 1978, certain rights and entitlements of trade unions and their members are preserved. All employees have the right to join and (subject to lawful closed shop agreements) to refuse to join a trade union. Also, they have the right to take part in trade union activities outside actual working hours on their employer's premises, and, by arrangement or agreement, to leave their work for that purpose. The enforcement of these rights is closely allied with the matter of unfair dismissal: an interference with them may lead to a claim for compensation in an industrial tribunal. In addition, trade union representatives have the statutory right to a reasonable amount of time off work to carry out their functions. The matter is governed by an official Code of Practice.

All these rights apply at sea.

11. Discrimination

There are three relevant Acts of Parliament on discrimination. The Equal Pay Act 1970 provides for men and women employed on the same work to receive the same pay and conditions of service. That Act did not come into force until 1975: it was brought into effect (and somewhat amended) by the Sex Discrimination Act 1975, which provides for the equal treatment of men and women in several fields, among them employment. The Race Relations Act 1976 represents a structural change in race relations law so as to put it on a basis similar to that introduced in 1975 for sex discrimination. The Equal Pay Act, however, has not been applied to differences in pay and conditions between people of different races: that remains restricted to sex.

The Equal Pay Act has nothing to say on the question of whether women should be employed on any particular job, or whether they should be given the same promotion or training opportunities or even whether they should be made redundant on the same basis as the men. All those issues are for the Sex Discrimination Act. The Equal Pay Act only answers the question: *if* a man and a woman are doing the same job, what terms should they get? The answer is, of course, that they should get the same, not only (as the title of the Act implies) in respect of pay, but also in respect of every other contractual term of employment.

The crucial question is what constitutes the same job. The Act speaks of "like work" and it is clear that the proper approach is to pay attention to what is actually done by the persons under comparison. Skills or qualities that are not actually used or put into practice are not relevant. The question is much easier if there has been a job-evaluation exercise. Provided that exercise is not of itself discriminatory, the rating adopted by it will answer the question.

A woman employed on like work with a man is entitled to the same pay and conditions and may enforce her right by complaint to an industrial tribunal. The employer may, by way of defence, justify the differential by proving a "material difference" between the two cases under comparison. This finds a place for the commonly accepted differentials based upon age, length of service, paper qualifications, quality of work, etc.

The Equal Pay Act applies also to claims by men.

The Sex Discrimination Act is wider in application. It applies to treating people (men or women) less favourably on the ground of sex, both directly and indirectly, by imposing a condition or requirement which it is advantageous to meet and which is such that more of one sex than of the other can comply. Indirect discrimination (which could include height requirements and, indeed, qualifications—there are many more certificated male master mariners than female) must be justified irrespective of sex. The burden is placed on the employer. The occasions of discrimination in employment run from the arrangements made for selection for the job, through training, promotion, etc., during employment, to discipline and dismissal at the end. The Sex Discrimination Act can thus cover the same ground as the Equal Pay Act. Some overlap is avoided by the provision that the Sex Discrimination Act is not to apply to claims for contractual money entitlements—wages.

The Sex Discrimination Act also applies to discriminating against the married on account of their marital status, and to discriminating against men.

The Sex Discrimination Act permits discrimination on eight closely-defined occasions where sex is declared to be a "genuine occupational qualification". There are only two of those eight occasions which could have any application to shipping. For a "living-in" job—and employment on board a ship certainly requires that the employee live in—sex is a genuine occupational qualification if the place is not equipped with separate sleeping or sanitary facilities and it is not reasonable to expect the employer to provide such. Clearly, the last part is crucial. Secondly, there is an exception where the job "is likely to involve the performance of duties outside the United Kingdom in a country whose laws or customs are such that the duties could not, or could not effectively, be performed by a woman". This might have limited application.

Breach of the Sex Discrimination Act is primarily a matter for individual complaint—generally leading to compensation—by the individual in an industrial tribunal. There is, however, an Equal Opportunity Commission set up by the Act whose function is not only to conduct investigations and keep the operation of the legislation under review, but to give assistance to individual complainants where necessary and, when the discrimination is persistent and in a number of other specified situations, take direct proceedings itself. These direct proceedings begin as formal investigations but can end with County Court injunctions against the discriminator.

Both the Sex Discrimination Act and the Equal Pay Act apply to maritime employment. The problem is that, like most United Kingdom Acts of Parliament, they do not apply outside territorial jurisdiction. This is met by section 10 of the Sex Discrimination Act (which also covers the Equal Pay Act). This provides that employment in a ship registered in Great Britain shall be regarded as employment in Great Britain unless the work is done wholly outside Great Britain. Other ships will be within the Act unless the work is done "wholly or mainly" outside Great Britain. In practical terms, the Acts are unlikely to apply to a foreign-registered ship, even if British owned, but will apply to British-registered ships so long as they touch British waters at some time.

The Race Relations Act 1976 is cast in the same form as the Sex Discrimination Act. There are some differences, however. There is no "living-in" or "foreign custom" exception: the occasions where race is allowed to be a genuine occupational qualification are very much more limited. The Act applies to the sea in the same terms as the Sex Discrimination and the Equal Pay Acts do, but there is an added limitation to its applicability. By section 9, the Act has no application to crew engaged abroad, whatever the ship's registration and wherever it plies. The exception also applies even where the crew, engaged abroad, is brought to England to join the ship.

12. Redundancy payments and unfair dismissal

Since 1965 those dismissed for redundancy—a decline in the employer's needs for work which the employee was employed to do—have been entitled to a lumpsum payment based upon their age and length of continuous employment. These claims are enforced by complaint to an industrial tribunal and are met, in the first instance, by the employer, who is entitled to claim a rebate from a fund created by a levy on employers and employees. The law is now to be found in the Employment Protection (Consolidation) Act 1978.

The major practical difficulty facing a maritime claimant for a redundancy payment may well lie in the need to show continuous employment with the same employer. The maritime industry is so organised that many employees have no great continuity with any particular employer. To make any claim, two years' continuous employment must be shown, and the amount of the payment rises in direct proportion to the number of completed years of continuous employment.

A claimant must have been dismissed for redundancy. Dismissal is widely defined so as to include the expiry and non-renewal of fixed-term contracts (of some significance to those with company service contracts) and the situation where the employee leaves because of his employer's conduct (usually understood as breach of contract by the employer) as well as the usual circumstances of termination, notice and dismissal for cause without notice. Redundancy is presumed, unless disproved by the employer.

Since 1971 dismissed employees have also had the right to complain of their dismissal and to have its fairness tested in an industrial tribunal. Such claims, where successful, generally lead to an award of damages. This part of the law is also now consolidated in the Employment Protection (Consolidation) Act 1978, Part V, as amended by the Employment Act 1980.

Continuity of employment is less of a problem here. One year's continuous employment is required before most claims can be made and, although part of the compensation will, like the redundancy payment, rise with completed years of continuous employment, some does not, being based upon consequential losses.

Once the claimant has shown that he was dismissed, it is for the employer to demonstrate to the tribunal what the reason for the dismissal was and that it was fair. The Act sets out five "fair" reasons: the capability or qualifications of the employee to do the job, redundancy, the conduct of the employee, that it would be illegal to continue his employment and "some other substantial reason of a kind such as to justify the dismissal". Certain reasons are always bad: interfering with the employee's guaranteed rights to join, not to join or participate in trade union activities and race or sex discrimination.

If the employer satisfies the tribunal that he had a good reason for dismissal, the matter does not rest there. The tribunal must then investigate whether, in all the circumstances, it was fair to dismiss or whether, for example, further warnings or goals for achievement should have been given or set, or whether the individual should have been transferred or demoted. Most important, the tribunal will be concerned to satisfy itself that a proper procedure was followed. Disciplinary procedures are the subject of an official Code of Practice, which, broadly, suggests that disciplinary procedures should be written, available and should contain known stages of operation: informal warnings, formal warnings, etc. At this level, by the Employment Act 1980, the burden of satisfying the tribunal is not on the shoulders of the employer. It is a matter for the tribunal to investigate.

The most usual remedy for unfair dismissal is compensation. This is made up of the Basic Award, calculated in accordance with the rules that govern the redundancy payment, and the Compensatory Award, which requires proof of loss brought about by the unfair dismissal. Both awards may be reduced by the tribunal on a variety of grounds: that the claimant contributed to his own losses, or that his behaviour would in fairness justify a reduction, for example.

The Employment Protection Act applies normally only to those employed in the United Kingdom. Those who "ordinarily work outside the United Kingdom" are excluded, but a person employed on board a ship registered in the United Kingdom is regarded as employed in the country unless *either* he works wholly outside the United Kingdom *or* he is not ordinarily resident here. There are also provisions designed to ensure that the fact that an individual was physically dismissed abroad should not prejudice him.

CHAPTER 16

CONFLICT OF LAWS

1. General

Conflict of laws is that part of the law of any country which deals with questions that are raised by cases which contain elements connecting them with other countries. If a Swedish national buys in Denmark an air ticket for a flight from London to Los Angeles with an American carrier and the aircraft crashes in Greenland, there are several competing systems of law available to answer the variety of legal questions that may arise from it. The principles upon which choice is to be made among those systems are the conflict of laws rules of a country.

Such questions can be put into two groups: which Courts are appropriate to refer the dispute to and which legal rules should be applied by those Courts to solve that dispute.

Conflict of laws rules are not part of international law: they are laws of a particular country with an international flavour and application. Therefore, the question of which Court is to take jurisdiction becomes, in any country's conflict of laws rules, the more comprehensible question of whether the Courts of that country will or will not accept jurisdiction in the case in question. In this respect, maritime contracts give rise to few problems in the United Kingdom, since, given the breadth of the jurisdiction accepted by the Admiralty Court, there are few cases in which, on grounds of principle, the English Court will refuse jurisdiction. Jurisdiction, therefore, is not regarded as a serious question of conflict of laws in this area, or indeed in any contractual or commercial matter.

The second question, which legal rules to apply, is much more significant. This is the question of "choice of law". The choice of law rule used by English Courts in contract questions is the doctrine of the "proper law of the contract". The proper law of the contract has been variously defined. The definitions vary partly by reference to the governing theories and notions of contract at the times when they were stated.

In the 19th century, in accordance with the dominant idea that contractors of full age and competent understanding were free to fix their rights and liabilities as they saw best, without restraint, the proper law of the contract was defined as the law intended by the parties as the law to govern their contract. If the parties had not made any express declaration of their intention in their contract, then the task of the Court was to discover from the contract as a whole and the surrounding circumstances what their intention must have been. In this century, that task is not seen as a search for evidence of an unexpressed intention, but rather as evidence of objective links between the contract and an available legal system or country.

In modern times we are left with three complementary rules: the first applies the expressed choice of the parties, the second allows a choice to be inferred from parallel clauses in the contract, such as arbitration clauses, and the third examines the circumstances of the contract to discover the legal system most closely connected with the transaction.

2. Express choice of law

In principle, the clear expression of the intention of the parties, contained in the contract, should always be effective as a choice of law. This is so even when the law chosen has otherwise no connection with the transaction at all. So, in *Vita Foods Products Inc.* v. *Unus Shipping Co. Ltd.* [1939] A.C. 277, a New York company shipped herrings on board a Nova Scotian-registered, Nova Scotian-owned ship for carriage from Newfoundland to New York. The vessel was stranded in Nova Scotia. The contract, perhaps by oversight, contained an English choice of law clause. That was held to be effective. English law governed, despite the fact that it had no real connection of any kind with the carriage in question.

There are some limitations to this rule, however. The Courts will not allow a choice of law which is contrary to public policy. In practice, this means that the parties to a contract cannot avoid a mandatory rule of English law simply by expressing a foreign choice, for the purpose of evasion. On occasion, this has been put into statutory form. By section 22 of the Unfair Contract Terms Act 1977 an express choice of law is to be disregarded if either the purpose of the choice appears to be the evasion of the Act or if it is a consumer transaction within the terms of the Act and the consumer to be protected is a habitual resident of the United Kingdom.

Additionally, some judges have stated their opinion that a choice of law that was in a general sense not made in good faith would be disregarded.

The express choice of law is not always very clear. It may be that it is unintelligible: if that is so, then it will be disregarded. In *Compagnie d'Armement Maritime S.A.* v. *Compagnie Tunisienne de Navigation S.A.* [1971] A.C. 572, a voyage charter-party was adapted for use as a contract for the carriage of a large bulk of crude oil by several unspecified ships. One clause of the charter-party stated that the governing law was to be the law of the flag of the carrying ship: but no single ship was contemplated, and no vessel was specified. For some of the judges involved in the case that was enough to justify disregarding that choice of law clause. It had no meaning.

3. Inferred choice of law: Arbitration clauses

Most maritime contracts contain an arbitration clause. This device enables the parties to submit their differences to a system of settlement that is generally regarded as quicker and cheaper than the Courts, and closer to the commercial expertise shared by the parties. Arbitrators operate as do judges. They must apply the law to the case before them and reach a proper conclusion. Their findings can, by appropriate procedure, be passed upon by a regular Court which will correct any errors of law. A reference to an arbitrator, then, is very similar to submitting to a Court's jurisdiction.

London arbitration clauses are common even in contracts that have no connection with England or any other part of the United Kingdom. The reason is simply that there is an available expertise in London which businessmen sometimes wish to use. The argument is that by choosing an English arbitrator the parties have implicitly chosen English law. That is not to say that an arbitrator is incapable of applying any legal system but his own. It is rather to say that by submitting to his jurisdiction some preference for the substantive rules applicable there has been expressed also.

The argument is often accepted—see *N.V. Kwik Hoo Tong Handel Maatschappij* v. *James Finlay & Co. Ltd.* [1927] A.C. 602. It is not, however, invariably conclusive. In *Compagnie d'Armement Maritime S.A.* v. *Compagnie Tunisienne de Navigation S.A.*, mentioned in the last section, an adapted voyage charter-party was used as a contract for the carriage of a considerable volume of crude oil owned by a Tunisian company, by a French shipowner in "tonnage owned, controlled or chartered" by that shipowner, from La Skhirra to Bizerta, two ports in Tunisia. The contract was in the English language and contained a London arbitration clause. The arbitrator held that French law applied and he was upheld by the Court. The arbitration clause, in these circumstances, could not be said to imply a choice of law. It was therefore relegated to the status of one factor among many in discovering the "closest connection" as the basis of the proper law of the contract.

4. The objective proper law of the contract

It is not possible to be dogmatic on the question of the weight that may be given to different relevant factors in the search for an objective proper law. The Court (or arbitrator) is seeking the closest connection. The place where the contract is made, the place where the contract is to be performed, the style and language of the contract, the permanent residence or the nationality of the parties, the place of arbitration and the place of payment and currency of payment of the price, charter-hire or freight are all from time to time relevant. In most cases, the factors build up in an obvious way.

One factor to which particular weight has traditionally been given is the flag of the carrying vessel. There is much old authority for the proposition that, at least when other factors are balanced, the law of the flag should govern. It would, however, be unwise to lay down any general principle. Some contracts provide expressly that the contract shall be governed by the law of the flag of the carrying ship. Such a term would operate as an express choice of law clause.

5. Proof of foreign law

In English Courts, foreign law is treated as a matter of fact, to be proved by appropriate evidence. The evidence normally accepted is the testimony of a practical expert in the system in question—a foreign lawyer in practice. If foreign law cannot be proved, or cannot be proved satisfactorily, it is presumed to be the same as English law.

6. Judgments in foreign currency

Until relatively recently it was accepted that because an English Court could only execute judgments in sterling, debts and damages had to be expressed in sterling at the date which in general governs an action, the date of the writ. In *Miliangos* v. *George Frank (Textiles) Ltd.* [1976] A.C. 443, the House of Lords decided that this was no longer the case and awarded execution of a debt owed in Swiss francs with a conversion date of the date of execution. This principle also applies to claims for damages for breach of contract (see *Federal Commerce & Navigation Co. Ltd.* v. *Tradax Export S.A.* [1978] A.C. 1) and even damages for torts (see *The Despina R.* [1978] 3 W.L.R. 804) if the losses are appropriately considered to have been suffered in that foreign currency.

CHAPTER 17

SEAWORTHINESS

1. The function of seaworthiness in maritime law

Seaworthiness is an idea that is fundamental to maritime law. The purpose of a merchant ship is to carry her cargo, whether that cargo be goods or passengers, and her crew, safely from her port of departure to her destination. A vessel that is fit for that task is seaworthy, one that is not is unseaworthy.

It must also be clear that this idea of seaworthiness is significant in several different legal contexts. First, and perhaps most obviously, the shipper of cargo has a distinct interest in the question of whether the ship in which his goods are to be placed is fit to take them from the port of loading to the port of discharge. It follows that the seaworthiness of the ship will be an important factor in fixing the legal liabilities and rights of cargo owner and shipowner in the law of carriage of goods by sea. Again, and also in the commercial area, a hull or cargo underwriter has an interest in whether the vessel he is insuring, or by which the goods he is insuring are to be carried, is or is not fit for the voyage on which he is taking a risk. Thus the seaworthiness of the vessel is a matter of some importance between underwriter and assured.

Finally, there is a public interest in ensuring that British ships are generally fit for their purpose. The history of the control of the safety of shipping is long and the legal provisions applicable to ships are, as a result, complicated. However, underpinning the system is the basic obligation imposed upon ships by the Merchant Shipping Acts, that which prohibits the sending to sea of an unseaworthy ship.

The first of these three areas is of greatest interest to shipbrokers and we will concentrate most attention upon that. The others will, however, be briefly mentioned.

2. A general definition of seaworthiness

Given the different contexts in which the idea of seaworthiness is legally important, it might well be asked whether it is at all possible to give a general definition of the term. There is high judicial authority for the proposition that seaworthiness means the same thing in marine insurance as it does in the carriage of goods by sea. That must, in a general sense, be true. There can be few differences between the two types of case. A vessel suffering a defect which renders her unfit to carry a cargo safely to her destination is likely to be regarded as unfit by her insurers.

This must, however, be somewhat qualified. Although the ideas are the same, the circumstances in which those ideas are used differ. If a ship is insured for a voyage from A to B, the insurer's primary concern is whether she is reasonably fit at the commencement of the voyage to carry the sort of cargo which a vessel of her type might be expected to load, over that part of the world's oceans at that time of the year. A cargo owner, with a particular cargo to load on board that vessel at that time is specifically concerned that the ship is reasonably fit to accept his particular cargo. The emphasis of interest is different and it is at least conceivable that different answers might be given: the ship might be seaworthy for the purposes of her marine insurance policy and unseaworthy for her charter-party.

Nevertheless, it is possible to describe the matters which may be taken into account in the discussion of whether a ship, for whatever purpose is seaworthy.

Seaworthiness is a relative, not an absolute, concept. One case which illustrates this well is *Burges* v. *Wickham* (1863) 3 B. & S. 669, in which a ship which was known to be a river steamer was sent upon an ocean voyage. Seaworthiness in this context meant doing what reasonably could be done to render her as fit as possible for that voyage. The standards of ocean vessels were not to be applied in an unqualified way. More generally, it can be said that seaworthiness means that the ship is, in all the particular circumstances, *reasonably* fit for the purpose contemplated. Seaworthiness will, therefore, vary with the vessel, with the voyage, with the season, and with the cargo. A ship may be seaworthy for a summer voyage in one ocean with this cargo, but unseaworthy in another place, or with a different cargo, or in the winter.

It is not therefore sensible to attempt to define seaworthiness by listing the conditions which are necessary for the fitness of all ships for all possible voyages at all times. However, we may indicate the areas of attention which are likely to be important in the decision whether a particular ship is fit for a particular voyage.

A ship is a large and complicated piece of operating machinery. Seaworthiness must include the physical condition of the vessel. Her hull must be sound enough for the voyage contemplated and she must have sufficient and appropriate tackle, equipment, stores and supplies. Her engines must be similarly fit and there must be sufficient fuel. In examining a ship's fitness for a voyage, the Court's attention is directed to some extent to future eventualities. A ship with inadequate bunkers is in a sense seaworthy *now* but is not fit for any voyage which requires more fuel than she has: she may, therefore, be held unseaworthy. In more general terms, we may say that unseaworthiness can include latent defects which are likely to cause damage in the future: one old example was the presence of muddy water in a ship's boilers, which was likely to clog and foul the vessel's boiler tubes during the coming voyage.

On the other hand, a mere temporary defect will not render the ship unseaworthy, at least so long as the defect is of the sort that one can reasonably expect to be put right by the crew. So in *Steel* v. *State Lines* (1877) 3 App. Cas. 72, a porthole was left open. The case is not satisfactory, since the facts were never established to the satisfaction of the Court, but it seems that such an error would not usually be enough to render the vessel unseaworthy.

The vessel must be properly manned. She must have enough officers and crew members, and they must be competent (see *Hongkong Fir Shipping* v. *Kawasaki Kisen Kaisha* [1962] 2 Q.B. 26). She must carry pilots when required. It may also be relevant that the crew was not properly instructed as to the vessel, or the voyage, in question. In *Standard Oil Co. of New York* v. *Clan Line Steamers Ltd.* [1924] A.C. 100, a ship's ballast tanks were emptied and she capsized. Vessels of that construction, turret ships, were likely to do that if the tanks were emptied when they were carrying homogeneous cargoes but not if they were carrying a variety of goods. The master, although generally competent, and experienced in turret ships, had not been specifically instructed of this particular risk. The ship was held unseaworthy.

The ship must also be of a type and construction that is reasonably fit for the voyage contemplated. There is less in this point than might be apparent, since in most contexts the type and age of the ship is known to the parties who are in dispute and the question is much more whether *this* ship is reasonably fit *as a vessel of this type* than it is whether vessels of this type are fit to sail the seas.

The ship's documents should be in order and, although minor failings can clearly be tolerated, a ship so badly documented that she is, on that account, unlikely to be able to complete her voyage, may be considered unseaworthy for that reason.

The vessel must also be reasonably fit to receive the cargo contemplated. Further, the poor stowage of the cargo may render her unseaworthy. She may simply be overloaded, or there may be deck cargo which interferes with safe navigation, or the cargo may simply be inexpertly stowed so as to affect stability.

There may, of course, be other factors. The list of relevant areas of examination cannot be closed. So long as the argument can be made that, on *this* account, the vessel was not reasonably fit for the contemplated voyage, an argument has been made that she was not seaworthy.

3. Carriage of goods by sea

Cargo ships are designed to carry goods by sea: generally speaking, those goods will not belong to the owner or operator of the ship. Of course, a trader may build or acquire a vessel for the exclusive purpose of carrying his own goods, but when this occurs, it presents us with few legal problems. There cannot be a conflict of interest.

When shipowner and cargo owner are different persons, they necessarily have conflicting interests. This may become a legal conflict when carriage fails; when the goods have not arrived safely at their destination. It is at this point that the question of seaworthiness may be raised. The cargo owner may claim that the loss was due to the unseaworthiness of the vessel. The shipowner may seek to show that it was not so, or, if it was, that his legal obligations with regard to seaworthiness have nonetheless been complied with.

A shipowner's legal obligations with respect to seaworthiness will vary depending upon the type of contractual relationship chosen by the parties to the carriage of goods by sea contract and upon the documentation used. These relationships are of the following broad types.

A ship may be chartered. There are three types of charter-party. The first, the charter by demise, need not concern us greatly here. A charter by demise is a contract whereby the charterer takes from the shipowner the widest powers of management and control. It is, in truth, the lease of a ship. The charterer by demise takes possession of the vessel, puts stores and bunkers on board her, employs the crew and uses her, broadly, as he thinks fit until the charter is done. That relationship is clearly more than the relationship between cargo owner and shipowner. For the purposes of the law of carriage of goods by sea, it has little significance.

A voyage charter-party is where all, or sometimes a substantial part, of the cargo of a ship is rented for a particular voyage. Here the charterer pays freight to the owner, expressed in terms of the vessel's capacity (so much per ton, or cubic foot of space, for example). The owner runs the ship, equips her, employs the crew, etc., and uses her to carry out his contract and conduct the ship on the contracted voyage.

A time charter-party is one where the charterer hires the ship for a determined period. Again, the running of the vessel remains the responsibility of the owner, but the ship will be used, within the general terms agreed in the charter-party, on the business of the charter. The charterer will expect to pay for the hire of the ship in some way which relates to the time he has bought: generally charter-hire at so much per month per deadweight ton, for example.

Charterers contract for the use of a vessel. Some charters will have enough cargo to fill the ship. Others will not. Again, there will be cargo owners with much less than a shipload of cargo to be carried. In these cases there will be other contracts for the carriage of goods by sea. These are contracts of affreightment, but that term can also quite properly be used of a cargo owner's charter-party.

Very often goods are carried by sea in the performance of an international sales contract. A manufacturer in the United Kingdom has sold some of his product to a buyer in Australia. The goods have to pass from England to Australia in pursuance of that contract. Such international deals pose practical commercial problems. They take time. Sellers, international or local, do not find it in their best interests to part with what they are selling before they are certain of the price. On the other hand, wise buyers want to see their purchase before they part with their money. If the goods are to be carried half way around the world, these quite legitimate needs are difficult to satisfy.

The solution worked out over the centuries of the development of maritime law is documentary sale. It may take different forms—the parties are, of course, free to deal with each other as suits them best—but under one common type, the c.i.f. contract, the seller will arrange transport and insurance, and pay the costs of these, place the goods on board a ship and look to the buyer for payment. When the seller has done his part, he will have acquired a set of documents. There will be an invoice, there will be a policy of insurance, there will be various Customs documents and, most important, there will be evidence of the contract of affreightment under which the goods were loaded on board the ship which will also be a receipt for the goods. This last is called a *Bill of Lading*.

A bill of lading therefore has three functions. It is a receipt for the goods by the shipowner, whose employee, the master of the vessel, received the goods on board and acknowledged their arrival. It is also evidence of the terms of the agreement under which the goods were transported: generally these terms appear on its back. Finally, it can be used as proof of entitlement to delivery of the goods at the port of discharge. It is legally recognised for this purpose. It is a *document of title* to the goods.

This bundle of shipping documents represents the cargo. If the cargo gets safely to its destination, the documents will ensure that the goods will be delivered to the correct person. If the cargo is lost overside, then the insurance can be used. These documents, then, can safely be exchanged for money. More than that, they can be dealt in, just like the goods themselves. They *represent* the goods. The advantages of a bill of lading are so clear that it may be attractive to a charterer who has filled the ship with his own goods to have a bill of lading issued to him, so as to be able to deal in the market with his cargo while it is in transit. In such a case, of course, the bill of lading is not a contract of affreightment—the charter-party is.

When looking at seaworthiness, therefore, in the context of carriage of goods by sea, we must examine it in three different circumstances: under a voyage charter-party; under a time charter-party; and under a bill of lading. The rights and liabilities are not the same in each case.

4. Seaworthiness under a voyage charter-party

A voyage charter-party may very well contain an express clause by which the owner guarantees the seaworthiness of the ship, or, at least, gives some relevant undertaking. It may be warranted "tight, staunch and strong, and in every way fitted for the voyage", to use the archaic terminology still often seen. Like any other contractual stipulation, such undertakings must be complied with precisely: if a vessel is warranted "tight" and is leaky, there is a breach of the warranty whoever may be at fault or not. What each clause means is a matter of interpretation in each case, but the overriding idea is the same in all, that the vessel should be fit for the work she is to do.

Voyage charter-parties are essentially contracts for a voyage from a port (or berth) of loading to a port (or berth) of discharge. The main thrust of the contract lies between these two points, when the cargo will be on board. However, ships chartered for a voyage do not have to be lying at their port of loading when the contract is made: they commonly are not. Thus an undertaking that the vessel is, to any extent, sea-worthy, given when the contract is made, is naturally understood to be an undertaking as to that time. This means, perhaps unexpectedly, that an express undertaking as to seaworthiness in a voyage charter-party will, unless the terms are clearly sufficient to cover further voyages, apply only to the voyage from wherever she is to the port of departure on the contracted voyage—the so-called preliminary voyage.

For the voyage itself, the subject and purpose of the charter-party, the obligation as to seaworthiness is implied into the contract. That is to say, that the law looks upon it as being included even though the parties have made no express provision. Of course, as a matter of general principle, it is open to the parties to amend the implied obligation by making express provisions, but the extent to which this is possible is to some extent limited by the Hague Rules. Under this international agreement the shipowner's right to limit his liabilities for the consequences of unseaworthiness and other matters is restricted, but the Rules' main impact is upon bills of lading not upon charter-parties. The matter is explained later.

The obligation to provide a seaworthy ship in a voyage charter-party is, at bottom, a duty to provide a ship fit for the contemplated voyage at the moment of departure. This means several things. First, the ship must be fit to receive the contemplated cargo—this is sometimes described as the obligation of "cargo-worthiness". What that cargo is depends upon the terms of the voyage charter-party. So long as the charterer proposes to load a cargo which, by those terms, he is entitled to load, he in turn is entitled to expect the vessel to be fit to receive it.

Second, the vessel must be fit for the voyage at the date set for her departure. There will be no breach of the seaworthiness obligation if the ship, although not presently fit to go to sea, can be made so before the voyage is due to start. She will be unseaworthy only if she cannot be so rendered by that date, or if the date for sailing arrives and it appears that she is not fit then.

Third, the seaworthiness of the ship after the voyage begins is generally not a matter for which the shipowner takes legal responsibility under a voyage charter-party. It would, indeed, be very hard if the owner were to be held liable because his perfectly good ship suddenly, through no fault, neglect or event for which he was responsible, became unseaworthy while on voyage. It would not be a proper imposition of strict liability. However, the *likelihood* of the vessel being able to complete her voyage *is* a relevant consideration. A ship, in her port of departure, which is in such a state that, although she is *now* perfectly capable of starting on the voyage, yet suffers from some defect which, unless remedied, is likely to prevent its successful completion, is *presently* unseaworthy.

As we have explained, seaworthiness is not an absolute concept. The proper standard to be applied in voyage charter-parties is that appropriate to the "reasonably prudent uninsured shipowner". If such a character would not, in the opinion of the Court, have sent that ship to sea on that voyage with that cargo, then the ship is unseaworthy.

The effect of unseaworthiness in a voyage charter-party is not always simply stated. The charterer, it is true, may refuse to load his cargo on board a ship which, at the port of loading, is clearly unseaworthy and cannot, by the date of sailing, be rendered reasonably fit to carry his cargo on the contemplated voyage. However, seaworthiness is a wide-ranging notion, and may consist of a variety of defects, several of them minor in themselves. It is often not possible to give a clear answer.

The general law of contract gives the innocent party two rights when the terms of the contract have been broken. In all cases he may sue for damages—money compensation intended to make good the financial loss suffered by him by reason of the breach by the other party. In addition, when the breach is more serious, the innocent party may throw up the whole contract. In such a case, he is said to "rescind" or to "repudiate further liability". The damages he is entitled to then are such as will compensate him for the loss of the bargain which he (justifiably) has given up.

The difference between these two remedies may be crucial. We may have to answer practical questions such as whether the charterer may refuse to load, may refuse to pay, or may inform the owner that he is no longer interested in the successful completion of the voyage. If he is not entitled to do these things, then he must accept the bad performance of the shipowner and may only recover damages to make good the loss he has suffered thereby. In practice, it is likely the only useful way in which a charterer might rescind a voyage charter-party on account of the unseaworthiness of the ship is by refusing to load cargo—the simple example quoted above. The actual possibilities of taking action in respect of unseaworthiness not discovered until *after* the voyage has begun are not great. Further, the sufferer of a serious breach of contract is not *obliged* to rescind: he may decide to affirm and make the best of it, claiming damages for the losses he has suffered at the end. Unless he takes fairly swift action to rescind when he *is* entitled, the Courts are likely to hold that he has implicitly decided upon the second option—affirming, carrying on and suing for damages later. So by delay he loses his right.

The central question is, however, which breaches justify rescission? At one time the approach favoured by the Courts was the categorisation of terms in accordance with their importance to the contract as a whole. Such important terms were variously described. They might be called "conditions" (as against "warranties") or "fundamental terms". Whatever terminology was used, the approach was the same: a condition or fundamental term was a term so important to the contract that breach of it would render performance substantially different from that which was expected. If this be adopted, then seaworthiness, obviously important, seems likely to be accounted a condition.

However, because of the variety of factors relevant to seaworthiness this approach had obvious limitations. It is now established that an alternative approach is proper with regard to the implied obligation of seaworthiness (see *Hongkong Fir Shipping* v. *Kawasaki Kisen Kaisha* [1962] 2 Q.B. 26). This does not categorise terms generally and for all eventualities. It rather concentrates upon the effects of the breach and asks the question whether, in the light of the breach or breaches that have occurred, it is now possible for the party in breach to render a performance which is not substantially different from that contemplated by the contract.

The practical result of this is that except in very serious cases of unseaworthiness, immediately apparent before loading, the charterer is not entitled to throw up the charter-party but must carry on with it and may sue for damages to make good his losses caused by the shipowner's breach.

5. Seaworthiness under a time charter-party

Under a time charter-party, the parties are not so much interested in the capability of the vessel to complete a particular operation with success as they are that the ship is generally fit to go to sea. Time charters usually state a time and a place where the ship will be made available to the charterer. This is the "port" of delivery (though it need not be a port). The owner is impliedly obliged to have the vessel at the port of delivery at the agreed time in a seaworthy state. However, at this point, it must be obvious that the contents of the seaworthiness obligation are likely to be less than in similar circumstances with a voyage charter-party. The charterer under a simple time charter-party cannot claim that the fitness of the vessel be judged against the special requirements of any voyage that he and the owner had in contemplation when the charter was made.

Of course, in reality, the time charter form is often used for transactions where it is clear to both parties that the ship is to be used within precisely defined limits. Again, the contract may be the hybrid consecutive voyage charter-party, which, though in form a time charter-party, is expressed to be for a number of defined voyages, with, perhaps, even the cargo specified. In such cases the obligation of seaworthiness grows. The vessel must be reasonably fit to carry out the agreed obligations.

If the owner provides a ship at the port of delivery which is manifestly unseaworthy and cannot be easily rendered seaworthy before she is due to be delivered under the contract, the charterer may refuse to accept delivery. That is, in law, the breach is treated as a breach of condition.

Once the charter has begun to run, the question of seaworthiness is less easy. In time charters, charterer and owner generally split the responsibilities for running the vessel. Usually, the owners will remain responsible for crewing the ship, for providing her stores, for arranging insurance. The charterer will be responsible for bunkers and for the incidentals of running the vessel, such as dock dues. These different obligations will be set out in the charter. One of these obligations is that the vessel will be maintained "in an efficient state" and that is a duty of the owner. It follows that if, during the currency of the charter, it is alleged that the ship ceased to be seaworthy, the matter becomes one of establishing that this state of affairs (if indeed it existed) was attributable to a breach by the owner of his obligations under the contract. This may be extremely complicated and involve the close examination of events and alleged defects—as to the physical condition of the ship, the qualities of her crew, the supplies, etc.

In these circumstances it is very difficult to ascertain the seriousness of the breach or breaches of contract, if any there be, covered by an allegation of unseaworthiness. The leading case on the matter, *Hongkong Fir Shipping* v. *Kawasaki Kisen Kaisha* [1962] 2 Q.B. 26, would establish that the charterer is only entitled to pull out of a time charter-party if the breach or breaches of contract, when taken together, are such as to render the continued performance of the contract impossible: to use a legal phrase, are such as to render the contract frustrated. In other cases he may only sue for damages.

6. Seaworthiness under a bill of lading

Except when a bill of lading is issued by a shipowner to a charterer of a ship, which may occur if the charterer wants to take advantage of the fact that the bill will be treated as a document of title to the goods shipped, and therefore enable him to deal in those goods while they are in transit, a bill is a contract of carriage of goods. It must, therefore, be treated in the same way as a charter-party when in respect of the obligation of seaworthiness.

There is an implied obligation that the ship will be reasonably fit to carry the goods described in the bill of lading to the destination named in the bill. This obligation is an obligation which is applied and tested at the commencement of the voyage. It is, therefore, similar in extent to the obligation of seaworthiness in voyage charter-parties, which has already been described.

In addition, because the bill of lading is a contract, it is, in principle, open to the parties to alter, extend or restrict this obligation as they think fit. However, the use of bills of lading by shipowners to limit or restrict their liabilities was one of the main factors which led to international action and the production of international standards of contracting governing carriage of goods by sea. These standards, the Hague Rules and, more recently, the Hamburg Rules, operate through bills of lading and are discussed below.

7. Exceptions and limitations: The Hague Rules and the Hamburg Rules

In olden times the carrier of goods by sea was placed under extremely heavy liabilities. He was regarded as a "common carrier" and common carriers, for historical reasons, were made in law strictly responsible for the safe delivery of the goods entrusted to their care, with few exceptions. In particular, the common carrier by sea was absolutely responsible for the seaworthiness of the vessel carrying the goods.

Carriers met this problem by using the freedom which the law gave them to make whatever contracts they chose, which they could persuade their customers to accept, by reducing to an absolute minimum their obligations. This produced certain problems. However much it could be argued that the carrier excluding or reducing the high level of his legal liability was imposing nothing on his immediate customer (who, in theory at least, could bargain as well as the shipowner), nevertheless, if the contract of carriage was to take effect in a bill of lading, that bill could be negotiated and dealt in. A subsequent holder of the bill, who would not be in a position to exert his influence in the settling of contractual terms, would be fixed by the agreement originally made by shipper and carrier.

This sort of debate led to the Hague Rules, which were first adopted in this country in the Carriage of Goods by Sea Act 1924. Improvements have been carried out to the rules over the years and the current governing statute is the Carriage of Goods by Sea Act 1971, which came into force in 1977. In 1978 a further conference was held in Hamburg and that conference produced a new set of rules, the Hamburg Rules. The Hamburg Rules are not yet in force and it may be many years before they are. Indeed, they may never be. They will be considered at the end of this section.

The Hague Rules are essentially applicable to bills of lading. When the carriage is simply by charter-party, and no bills are issued, the Rules have no application. If the shipper charters the vessel and fills her with his own cargo but has bills issued to himself, then, as we have already said, the contract of carriage is still the charter-party, not the bills of lading. The bills are issued for the shipper's convenience: so that he can, by negotiating them to a purchaser, trade with the cargo even before it arrives at its destination. In such a case, the Hague Rules only apply from the moment that the bills govern the relations "between a carrier and the holder" of the bills. In other words, when the bills have been negotiated and are now held by a purchaser from the charterer, the holder's rights are governed not by the charter, which he did not make, but by the bill of lading, which, in law, is "negotiable" and can be transferred, with its rights and entitlements, to others. A holder is in no different position from that of the non-charterer shipper.

The Hague Rules apply compulsorily to contracts of carriage by sea where the port of shipment is in the United Kingdom. They may be adopted by the bill of lading and incorporated into contracts where the port of shipment is outside the United Kingdom. The function of these requirements, if considered in relation to the similar legislation enacted by other nations who ratified the Hague Rules, is to ensure a uniform international application of the rules, with each case being decided by the law governing the State of the port of shipment.

The Rules do not apply to the carriage of live animals or deck cargo, provided that such carriage is declared upon the bill of lading. The cases establish that this exception will not apply to a simple "liberty" to carry on deck: the cargo must be declared as deck cargo in the bills (*Svenska Traktor Aktiebolaget* v. *Maritime Agencies (Southampton) Ltd.* [1953] 2 All E.R. 570). Again, it is always possible for parties to a deck cargo or live animal bill of lading to incorporate the Hague Rules expressly.

The main purpose of the Hague Rules is to establish a regime of limited liability for carriage by sea. Thus they establish a general level of liability, expressed as a maximum sum per package or per kilo of cargo, set out a list of "excepted perils" for the consequences of which the carrier is not liable at all, impose a limitation of action requirement that claims be made within one year from the date of delivery of the goods, and set out rules relating to the obligations with regard to care of cargo. The limitation of liability provisions, and those related to them, are dealt with elsewhere.

As regards seaworthiness, the Hague Rules abolish the old strict liability of the carrier for unseaworthiness. This is replaced by an obligation to "exercise due diligence" before the voyage and at its start to make the vessel seaworthy. This obligation covers the same ground as unseaworthiness: the carrier must use due diligence to make the ship fit for the voyage as well as to ensure that she is properly manned, equipped and supplied and that the vessel is fit for the safe stowage and carriage of the cargo in question. The standard of the obligation is clearly somewhat lower, however. It would seem to be established from the cases, however, that once unseaworthiness is proved, it is for the carrier to prove that he has exercised due diligence and that he will not easily demonstrate this simply by showing that the work was carried out by someone else. The responsibility is, in some sense, personal (see *Riverstone Meat* v. *Lancashire Shipping* [1961] A.C. 807).

Together with this treatment of unseaworthiness proper under the Hague Rules, we should notice that the Rules impose an obligation upon the carrier to "load, handle, stow, carry, keep, care for and discharge" the cargo "properly and carefully".

The Hamburg Rules, which are not yet in force, have the aim of effecting several changes. One is the reworking of the mechanism of limitation of liability in order to deal with the legal questions raised by the practice of palletising and containerising cargo. Another is to ensure a wider application of the compulsory effect of the Rules by requiring that they be applied to other carriages, where, for example, the destination lies in a contracting State. In respect to seaworthiness, however, the most important proposed change is the discarding of "due diligence" in favour of a standard which would make the carrier liable for loss or damage occurring during carriage, unless he affirmatively proves that he and his employees took all measures he reasonably could to avoid such loss.

8. Seaworthiness in policies of marine insurance

In policies of marine insurance, by section 39 of the Marine Insurance Act 1906, seaworthiness is a matter for warranty. The word "warranty" has a peculiar—and different—meaning in marine insurance from that which it enjoys in the general law of contract. A warranty in an insurance policy, far from being a clause of secondary importance, as it is in other contracts, is a condition upon which further liability depends. Failure of an insurance warranty is grounds for the insurer—the underwriter —repudiating liability and refusing to meet the claim. Indeed, the strict position is even harsher than this. Unless the insurer chooses to waive the breach of warranty, he is automatically relieved of liability as from the date of the breach, although he remains liable for claims arising before.

Like charter-parties, marine insurance policies are of two main kinds. Voyage policies attach for a particular described voyage. Time policies for a particular period of time. In voyage policies there is, by virtue of the Act, an implied warranty that the vessel will be "seaworthy for the purpose of the particular adventure insured" at the commencement of the voyage. If the voyage is to be completed in stages, then the obligation applies at the commencement of each stage. In addition, there is an implied warranty that the vessel be "port-worthy" if the policy attaches when she is in port, in respect of the risks of the port before the voyage begins. Seaworthiness means reasonably fit for the voyage, and it must mean much the same as in a voyage charter-party.

With time policies, there is no implied warranty of seaworthiness, but if the ship is sent to sea during the policy in an unseaworthy state "with the privity of the assured", then the insurer is not liable for any losses attributable to that unseaworthiness, although the policy remains in force. The shipowner—the assured—is "privy" to the act of sending the ship to sea in an unseaworthy state if the conditions giving rise to the state of unseaworthiness were known to him and it is shown that he was aware of the significance of those facts. Mere negligence by the shipowner is not enough to amount to "privity", but consciously shutting one's eyes to facts or the importance of facts will defeat an insurance claim based upon the unseaworthy state of the vessel (see *Compania Maritima San Basilio S.A.* v. *Oceanus Mutual Underwriting Association (Bermuda) Ltd., The Eurysthenes* [1976] 3 All E.R. 243).

That same case also establishes that membership of a P. & J Club amounts to a time policy within the meaning of the Marine Insurance Act. Thus, a club may validly refuse to meet the claims of a member who has "privily" sent his ship to sea in an unseaworthy state, at least as regards those claims that derive from the vessel's unseaworthiness.

There is no compulsion about seaworthiness liabilities in marine insurance. It is open to the parties to agree that unseaworthiness may have different consequences as regards their contract if they should so wish. A common form clause, often added to policies of the marine insurance, is the "seaworthiness admitted" clause which states simply that, as between insurer and assured, the seaworthiness of the vessel is admitted. The effect of this is that the implied warranty of seaworthiness, and the consequences of section 39 of the Marine Insurance Act 1906 on time policies, is defeated. The fact that the vessel may be unseaworthy will be of no significance in any claim made under a policy containing this clause.

9. Seaworthiness in public maritime law

It is a criminal offence for anyone to send a dangerously unseaworthy British ship to sea or to attempt to do so (Merchant Shipping (Safety Conventions) Act 1949, section 29). A ship is dangerously unseaworthy if her unseaworthiness is likely to endanger life. The offence is one of near-strict liability. It is not generally necessary for the prosecution to prove that it was committed knowingly, but a defence that all reasonable means were used to ensure that the ship was seaworthy or that it was, in all the circumstances, reasonable and justifiable to send her to sea unseaworthy is available. Both owner and master, or any other person responsible, may be prosecuted. The master of the ship, however, is only guilty if he knew of the unseaworthiness.

Any ship, British or foreign, may be detained for survey and examination in any British port, if alleged to be unsafe, either from defects in machinery or hull, or from loading or from undermanning (Merchant Shipping Act 1894, section 459). If found to be unsafe, the detention may be continued until the defects are remedied.

Many other provisions are relevant to seaworthiness. There are provisions relating to certification and survey upon registration. There are particular rules relating to safety equipment, manning, radio rules, construction rules and rules governing load lines. The aim of all can be described as the creation and maintenance of seaworthiness in ships, but it is not within our present scope to cover that in detail.

CHAPTER 18

DAMAGES IN SHIPPING CONTRACTS

1. General rules

The purpose of the award of damages for breach of contract is to give the innocent party that to which he was entitled by the contract that has been broken. Therefore, in principle, he is entitled to the equivalent, in money, to what he should have got from the performance of the contract. The Courts will attempt to put him where he should have been had the contract been fully carried out.

To this general principle certain qualifications must be added. First, the innocent party must mitigate his loss. With few exceptions, he must act in a reasonable way to reduce his losses and avoid waste. He may not sit tight and watch the damages mount. He must recharter the ship or find more cargo space for his goods. Again, the purpose of damages is the compensation of the injured, not the punishment of the guilty. So, although the parties may, and often do, fix the compensation in advance by way of liquidated damages clauses (like demurrage clauses) the Courts will not enforce penalties designed to deter breach. Finally, damages will not be awarded for losses too remote from the breach. A party in breach of contract is not to be held liable for unexpected or unreasonably distant consequences of his actions.

The consequence of these qualifications is that it could be said that damages represent an estimate of the *reasonable* costs of the breach of contract. What follows is a detailed examination of the rules in relation to contracts of carriage of goods by sea. First, however, a more detailed examination of the rules of remoteness, mitigation and penalties is necessary.

2. Remoteness

Traditionally, the remoteness rule for breach of contract was stated in a two-fold formulation. For many years, the leading case on the subject was *Hadley* v. *Baxendale* (1854) 9 Ex. 341, in which the carrier (by land) of a mill-shaft was held not liable for the loss of profits caused by its late delivery. He had no way of knowing that the delay would have that effect. Alderson, B., said that damages for breach of contract

> ". . . should be such as may fairly and reasonably [be] considered either arising naturally, i.e., according to the usual course of things, from such breach of contract itself, or such as may reasonably be supposed to have been in the contemplation of both parties, at the time they made the contract, as the probable result of the breach of it".

Until relatively recently, this statement was interpreted as providing for two rules: one covering damages "naturally" arising and the other covering "extra" damages, only recoverable when it could be said that the parties "had them in contemplation"—i.e. knew of the possibility of their arising.

In *Czarnikow* v. *Koufos* [1969] 1 A.C. 350, however, this approach was discarded. Looking at all the circumstances, the question to be answered is whether, in the light of those circumstances and the parties' knowledge of them, it was "not unlikely" that the loss at issue would result from such breach. Specific knowledge of a particular loss-producing circumstance, still less acceptance by the party in breach of liability for it, is not required. So, in the *Czarnikow* case, a cargo of sugar was nine days late at its destination, Basrah, and, in the meantime, another cargo of sugar had arrived whose sale had depressed the market. The carriers were held liable for the difference between the market price of the cargo on the day it arrived and that prevailing on the day it should have arrived, despite the fact that neither they nor the cargo owners could have known of the arrival of the other ship. Losses due to fluctuations in the market—even gross fluctuations attributable to one identifiable cause—were not unlikely consequences of delay.

In practical terms, a very common situation raising remoteness questions is when the innocent party loses an expected profit on an existing forward sale. Clearly, in a broad sense, the market profitability of his goods is a correct head of damage, even when the party in breach has no knowledge of that sub-sale. Merchants have their goods carried so that they can sell them profitably in the marketplace at their destination. So, in most cases, it is easy to see that, although a particularly lucrative sale cannot appear in the plaintiff's damages unless the contract was made on that basis, general market losses are recoverable. Some cases pose problems. One such is *Czarnikow* v. *Koufos*, described above. Another is *The Arpad* [1934] P. 189, where the only available evidence of the market price of the commodity in question was the price obtained on the forward sale.

3. Mitigation

The general application of the mitigation rule causes few problems. If a charterer fails to load a cargo, the shipowner must seek a cargo to fill his ship. If he does not, he cannot thereby increase his damages and claim the full amount of the freight. He will be awarded the difference between the contract rate and the market rate. If there is no difference there is no loss and damages will be nominal.

There is one exception to this general rule. Breach of contract usually occurs when a party subject to an obligation under the contract fails to carry it out, or fails to carry it out completely. It is, however, also possible to break a contract before the time for performance has arrived, by repudiating future liability. By saying, in short, "I will not perform". When this occurs, the innocent party may accept that behaviour as a serious breach, accept it as bringing the contract to an end, and claim damages there and then. No great problem arises if he takes that course. However, he is not obliged to act thus. He may, if he can, continue with the contract, wait for the date for performance, and sue then. This can have the effect of greatly increasing the damages. In the leading case, a firm of advertising agents refused to accept a cancellation of the contract, placed the advertisements for three years and sued for the full contract price. They were successful (*White and Carter (Councils) Ltd.* v. *McGregor* [1962] A.C. 413). However, this option is only open in practice in two circumstances. First, where the innocent party can continue to perform without the active co-operation of the party in breach, as in *White and Carter (Councils) Ltd.* v. *McGregor*, and second, where the contract may be enforced by an order of specific performance. Commercial contracts are not generally specifically enforceable, and few shipping contracts are as "one-sided" as the advertising contract in *White and Carter (Councils)* v. *McGregor*.

A similar issue might be seen to arise in a more common situation. For a breach of contract, damages are always available. For a serious breach of contract, such as renders future performance different from that expected, the innocent party also has the right to "accept the breach" and bring the contract to an end. He is not obliged thereto. If he wishes to continue he may. This may have the effect of increasing the losses, and therefore the damages. It is established that the innocent party is not obliged to bring the contract to an end for such a breach. The mere breach does not bring it to an end by itself. In *Suisse Atlantique Societe d'Armement Maritime S.A.* v. *N.V. Rotterdamsche Kolen Centrale* [1967] 1 A.C. 361, the charterer in a consecutive voyage charter-party consistently delayed the ship, in breach of contract. The owner was entitled to continue with the voyages and was not obliged to call off the charter-party.

Such exceptions are only apparent exceptions, however. The principle is intact.

4. Penalties, liquidated damages, demurrage and dispatch money

It is always open to the parties to a contract to specify the consequences of any breach. The advantages of so doing are clear. In the event of breach the innocent party is not put to the difficulty and expense of proving loss and claiming damages within the rules: he is entitled to the sum set forth in the contract on proof of the events conditioning entitlement. The party in breach may also be seen to benefit. He too is relieved of the expense of meeting a complicated claim, and in addition he is able to predict with precision the extent of his pecuniary responsibility for the breach in question.

Penalties, on the other hand, are not encouraged by the law. There is a general jurisdiction in the Courts to relieve parties to a contract from a penalty: variously defined but most simply as a sum of money set not in genuine pre-estimation of damages, but to encourage performance. It is sometimes a nice question whether a particular clause imposes a penalty or a sum by way of liquidated damages. In such a task, the Courts will look to the substance rather than the form and seek to establish the intention of the parties when the contract was made.

In shipping the most obvious candidate for consideration as a penalty is a demurrage clause. The function of a demurrage clause is not difficult to state. For the loading and unloading of a ship it is common to specify in the charter-party a number of "laydays". Laydays are the days allowed and expected for the completion of the job. (If no laydays are set out, then the work must be done with reasonable dispatch.) The contract may specify working days as laydays or weather working days (thus deducting days when work is not possible because of bad weather) or any other convenient description. When the laydays are used up, the charter-party then may (and usually will) provide for a further period of demurrage, during which the charterer is obliged to pay to the owner a set sum per day until the loading or unloading is complete. Demurrage may be agreed for an unlimited or, occasionally, for a limited period. If the ship is delayed beyond demurrage, then the owner may have a claim against the charterer for that delay. Such a claim is a claim for damages—damages for detention.

Demurrage clauses are only necessary in voyage or mixed charter-parties, where the owner's remuneration is expressed in terms of the cargo carried. In time charters where the freight relates only to time, demurrage is not relevant.

It is established by high authority, the House of Lords in the case of *Suisse Atlantique Societe d'Armement Maritime S.A.* v. *Rotterdamsche Kolen Centrale N.V.* [1967] 1 A.C. 361, that a demurrage clause is not a penalty but a genuine pre-estimate of damages, despite the fact that it is invariably set at a fixed sum per day and does not vary with any other circumstance.

5. Damages for failure to load

The charterer of a ship is under a duty to load a cargo in accordance with the charter-party then, if the shipowner's entitlement to freight depends, as it will under a voyage charter-party, upon the tonnage loaded, the primary measure of damages is the difference between the charter rate and the prevailing market rate. The shipowner, by way of mitigation, is expected to find another cargo and load it and has therefore lost his profit on that original charter-party. A different way of reaching a similar result, found in the older cases, is to allow the owner the loss of his profit on that charter—the freight less the cost of earning it—together with estimated profits on a substituted voyage.

If a charterer loads a less than full cargo then he pays damages for the shortfall. Since the owner has expended the money necessary to earn it (in earning freight for the cargo actually shipped) the usual measure of damages will in fact be the freight payable for the unshipped cargo. This is generally known as "deadfreight" and it may be expressly provided for in the contract: in such a case the deadfreight clause is a liquidated damages clause.

The charter-party may provide for a cargo of a particular description. If the charterer loads a cargo of a different description, the shipowner is entitled to damages for the difference between the market freight rate for the cargo actually shipped and the charter rate. If the market rate was not higher than the charter rate, the shipowner has suffered no loss and has no substantial claim.

Late loading is dealt with by clauses relating to laydays and demurrage. Outside demurrage clauses, the owner is entitled to damages for detention—the loss of his profits in the use of his ship for that period.

6. Damages for failure to carry or to carry safely

If the shipowner does not provide a ship to carry the charterer's cargo within the terms of the charter-party, the primary measure of damages will be the difference between the freight payable under the charter-party and the market rate. The charterer gets his loss of bargain. If the charterer has in fact chartered another ship, or has taken other action to have his cargo carried, then his expenses, if reasonable, will provide the base for the calculation of damages. If the cargo could not be carried to its destination, the measure of damages is the cost of replacing the goods by purchase in the destination, less the cost of transport and insurance and less the value of the goods actually owned in the place of shipment. The charterer gets his loss of trading profit in the market to which his goods were headed.

If the goods never arrive because the carrier loses them, the cargo owner is entitled to their value at the time and place of their arrival, less the cost of shipping—that is the freight. A similar approach is used for damaged goods: the measure of damages is the difference between the sound value of the cargo at the time and place of arrival, less the actual value of the damaged goods.

If the goods arrive late, then the measure of damages is the difference between their value at the date they did arrive and the date they should have arrived. Market fluctuations, even large unpredictable ones, are borne by the carrier.

7. Limitation, limitation clauses and exemption clauses

On general principle it is as open to the parties to limit liability as to fix it by appropriate clauses in the contract. On the same argument, that freedom should be extended to clauses exempting one or other party from liabilities also. Such limitation or exemption clauses are commonly used, usually to the benefit of the shipowner, in contracts of affreightment. They have, however, been subject to much legal restraint and qualification.

To consider clauses exempting a party from liability first, the Courts have for many years taken the view that they be regarded with great strictness. Thus, for them to be relied upon, it is necessary that they be clearly drawn and that the party whose rights are diminished by them have proper notice of them. Such requirements are usually satisfied in contracts for the carriage of goods by sea, but some particular points might be noticed.

As a matter of interpretation, exemption clauses will not be understood as exempting the carrier from liability when he is not carrying out the essential obligations of the contract. To hold otherwise would be to allow him to offer nothing, or very little, by way of legal obligation in return for payments made to him. Thus in *Glynn* v. *Margetson and Co.* [1893] A.C. 351, a cargo of oranges was to be carried from Malaga to Liverpool. The contract gave the carrier liberty to call at any port in the Mediterranean, the Black Sea and other places. However, when the vessel first proceeded east to Valencia before making for Liverpool, the shipowners were held liable for the deterioration of the fruit caused by the delay, despite the wide liberty. Again, in *Sze Hai Tong Bank Ltd.* v. *Rambler Cycle Co. Ltd.* [1959] A.C. 576, carriers who released the cargo without the production of a bill of lading, so that the shippers were never paid, were liable despite a clause exempting shipowners from liability after the goods had been discharged from the ship.

There are several ways of putting this rule. One would be to say that the carrier can only rely upon his exemption clause when carrying out the contract: not when deviating or failing in an essential obligation. Another would be to say that a clause in general terms will not be held to extend to breaches of contract which go to its root, or which are so fundamental as to render performance something substantially different from that which was expected. As a matter of ordinary business practicability it is unlikely that the drafting of a clause precise enough to cover these gross breaches of contract is possible and, if possible, the result is likely to be unacceptable.

The idea of fundamental breach was further developed. The Courts have on several occasions said that if a party is in fundamental breach of contract, he may not rely upon an exemption clause: such a rule is not a matter of interpretation, but of substance, In *Suisse Atlantique Societe d'Armement Maritime S.A.* v. *N.V. Rotterdamsche Kolen Centrale* [1967] 1 A.C. 361, however, the House of Lords decided, apparently, that such a consequence only ensued when the innocent party, when faced by fundamental breach, exercised his right to "accept the repudiation" and bring the contract to an end. If he chose not to do that but instead affirmed the contract, he was bound by the exemption clause. So in that case, a shipowner with a consecutive voyage charter-party who continued with the contract after many delays by the charterer, and so affirmed the contract, would have been bound by any exemption clause the contract contained. However, it has been pointed out in other cases that some breaches are so devastating in their consequences that to ask whether the innocent party has affirmed or repudiated is not sensible (*Harbutt's "Plasticine" Ltd.* v. *Wayne Tank & Pump Co. Ltd.* [1970] 1 Q.B. 447) and there is some authority for the view that, even after affirmation, the substantive rule still operates and the party in breach is precluded from reliance (*Wathes (Western) Ltd.* v. *Austin (Menswear) Ltd.* [1976] 1 Lloyd's Rep. 14). The matter is probably academic. In practical terms, whether the rule is seen as one of substance or of interpretation, it is highly unlikely that a party in fundamental breach will be able effectively to exempt himself from liability by reliance upon an ordinary exemption clause.

The right to exempt from liability is now covered, in the general law, by the Unfair Contract Terms Act 1977. This statute adopts a threefold approach to exemption clauses. It prohibits the exemption of liability for death or personal injury caused by the defendant's negligence, it restricts the right of the defendant to rely upon an exemption clause to exempt him from liability for other losses caused by negligence to occasions when it is "reasonable" to do so and it applies the same standard of reasonableness to reliance upon exemption clauses generally when the other party "deals as consumer or on the other's written standard terms of business". There are special provisions for charter-parties and contracts for the carriage of goods by sea. To such contracts the first provision applies: exemption of liability for death or personal injury caused by negligence is prohibited. As regards other exemption clauses, however, the protection can only be activated by a person "dealing as consumer". That phrase is defined by section 12 of the Act thus: a party deals as consumer if he does not make the contract in the course of business and the other party does so. In practice, therefore, the Unfair Contract Terms Act has little application to carriage of goods by sea. Most shippers ship cargo by way of business. Shipowners cannot exempt themselves from liability for death or personal injury caused by negligence, but such claims rarely, if ever, arise from contracts of affreightment.

By section 502 of the Merchant Shipping Act 1894, a shipowner is declared not to be liable for loss of or damage to goods by reason of fire on board the vessel, provided that the fire did not occur with his actual fault or privity. A carrier may, of course, bargain away his immunity and on occasion the terms of a contract of carriage by sea have been interpreted in the sense that this has been done. There is an equivalent provision, in the same section, for "gold, silver, diamonds, watches, jewels or precious stones" shipped without prior declaration of their nature and value. Additionally, section 448(2) of the same Act declares that there is no liability for dangerous goods shipped under a false description.

Contractual exemption of liability is traditionally effected by way of "excepted perils". The contract declares that no liability is accepted by the shipowner for losses caused by any one of a list of circumstances—commonly including act of God, enemies, piracy, barratry, perils of the sea, collision, negligence of the master and crew, etc.—provided that loss by such perils could not have been avoided by reasonable care and diligence by the shipowner. However, subject to the compulsory application of the Hague Rules (see later), freedom of contract prevails. Within the general limitations described above, a carrier who can find a shipper who will accept his terms may agree to carry on any contract he wishes—including "sole risk" terms.

Where the Hague-Visby Rules apply compulsorily, by virtue of the Carriage of Goods by Sea Act 1971, the picture is changed. That statute, it will be remembered, applies to carriage by a bill of lading. It thus does not apply to charter-parties, save when a bill has been issued and negotiated to a holder who is now enforcing. Nor does it apply to deck cargo or the carriage of live animals, and the English Act is restricted to outward ocean bills of lading, except where the Rules are expressly incorporated. The Rules regulate the matter of excepted perils. The only permitted excepted perils, where the Rules apply, are:

(a) Act, neglect, or default of the master, mariner, pilot, or the servants of the carrier in the navigation or in the management of the ship.

(b) Fire, unless caused by the actual fault or privity of the carrier.

(c) Perils, dangers and accidents of the sea or other navigable waters.

(d) Act of God.

(e) Act of war.

(f) Act of public enemies.

(g) Arrest or restraint of princes, rulers or people, or seizure under legal process.

(h) Quarantine restrictions.

(i) Act or omission of the shipper or owner of the goods, his agent or representative.

(j) Strikes or lock-outs or stoppage or restraint of labour from whatever cause, whether partial or general.

(k) Riots and civil commotions.

(l) Saving or attempting to save life or property at sea.

(m) Wastage in bulk or weight or any other loss or damage arising from inherent defect, quality, or vice of the goods.

(n) Insufficiency of packing.

(o) Insufficiency or inadequacy of marks.

(p) Latent defects not discoverable by due diligence.

(q) Any other cause arising without the actual fault or privity of the carrier, or without the fault or neglect of the agents or servants of the carrier, but the burden of proof shall be on the person claiming the benefit of this exception to show that neither the actual fault or privity of the carrier nor the fault or neglect of the agents or servants of the carrier contributed to the loss or damage.

Arguments on the application of this aspect of the Hague-Visby Rules resolve themselves into arguments about the causation of the loss. Whether it was truly attributable to one or other of the excepted perils or to the carrier's failure in his obligations, such as using due diligence to render the ship seaworthy, for example.

In addition to exemption of the shipowner's liability, there is law on the limitation of that liability. First, under section 503 of the Merchant Shipping Act 1894, as amended, (in particular by the Merchant Shipping (Liability of Shipowners and Others) Act 1958), shipowners, charterers, their employees and others, may limit liability in certain claims, including claims in respect of loss or damage to goods on board the vessel, by reference to the tonnage of the vessel. The matter is dealt with in greater detail elsewhere. Limitation under the statutes is not available if the loss occurred with the actual fault or privity of the shipowner. If the claim exceeds the notional fund created by applying the Rules, it is reduced: if there are several claims, they are reduced *pro rata*.

It is also possible to limit liability by contract. Under the Hague-Visby Rules, and therefore compulsorily where they are compulsory under the Carriage of Goods by Sea Act 1971, unless the nature and value of the goods have been declared before shipment and an appropriate insertion into the bill of lading made, liability is limited to 10,000 gold francs per package or 30 francs per kilo, whichever is the greater. It was partly a result of the difficulty in applying the "package" rule in modern times that the Hamburg Conference produced the new, but as yet unimplemented, Hamburg Rules. The new Rules clearly declare that pallets and containers, if that description is used in the bill of lading, are the "packages" for the purpose of limitation.

INDEX